Thanksgiving Dinner

Thanksgiving Dinner

KATHRYN K. BLUE
ANTHONY DIAS BLUE

HarperCollins*Publishers*

Parts of this book originally appeared in slightly different form in *Bon Appétit*.

FIRST EDITION

Designed by Helene Berinsky

Library of Congress Cataloging-in-Publication Data

Blue, Kathryn K., 1943–
   Thanksgiving dinner/Kathryn K. Blue, Anthony Dias Blue.—1st ed.
    p. cm.
   ISBN 0-06-016490-5
   1. Thanksgiving cookery. 2. Entertaining. I. Dias Blue, Anthony. II. Title.
TX739.2.T45B58 1990   89-26961

90 91 92 93 94 DT/RRD 10 9 8 7 6 5 4 3 2 1

For Caitlin, Toby, Jessica, and Amanda,
for whom we give thanks every day

Contents

It has seemed to me fit and proper that they should be solemnly, reverently and gratefully acknowledged as with one heart and one voice by the whole American people. I do, therefor, invite my fellow citizens in every part of the United States, and also those who are at sea and those who are sojourning in foreign lands, to set apart and observe the last Thursday of November next as a day of thanksgiving and praise to our beneficent Father who dwelleth in the heavens.

—Abraham Lincoln, October 3, 1863

Acknowledgments

We started this project because we love Thanksgiving. Now, after more than a year of Thanksgiving dinners, we still do. Not only that, we are still talking to each other and we still like turkey.

What made this such a pleasant experience was the excellent support we received from so many people. First and foremost we want to thank our dear Alice Nolan, who labored long and hard testing and tasting and giving us sound advice, while our administrative assistant, Jack Weiner, manned the phones and ran the office.

Special thanks to Diane Rossen Worthington, an accomplished cook, successful cookbook author, and good friend, who provided guidance and good ideas throughout the process; and to Susan Friedland, our editor, who administered motivation when needed and scoldings when deserved.

Thanks to all those who contributed ideas, recipes, and encouragement: Gertrud Blue, Daniel Boulud, Flo Braker, Daphne Bransten, JoAnn Coffino, Lyn Davis, Fran Deutsch, Patty Dinner, Barbara Folger, Meredith Frederick, Barbara Goldie, Laurie Burrows Grad, Muffie Graham, Paige Healy, Lois Jamart, Maddie Katz, Peggy Knickerbocker, Heidi Insalata Krahling, Martha Kropf, Liz Levy, Susan Lifrieri, Amanda Lyon, Peggi McGlynn, Sirio Maccione, Dinah Malkin, Fran Meiselman, Lee Monfredini, Joan Nathan, Drew Nieporent, Andy Pappas, Jonathan Parker, Cindy Pawlcyn, Debra Ponzac, Mary Powell, Alex Rosenblatt, Caryl Saunders, Bonnie Schmitz, Emmy Smith, Kit Snedaker, James Villas, Martha Pearl Villas, Clark Wolf, Sue Wollack, Sudie Woodson, and Rob Zaborny.

Also we appreciate the help we received from the California Turkey Board, Empire Kosher Poultry, National Turkey Federation, Ocean Spray, and Shady Brook Turkey Farms.

A Little History

The first Thanksgiving feast is reputed to have taken place in 1621 with the Pilgrims and some local Massachusetts Indians in attendance. Some historians give credit to the settlers at Jamestown, Virginia, because they celebrated the Harvest Home Festival, a traditional English autumnal rite, a few years before the Pilgrims.

The traditions of these colonial celebrations go back as long as men have cultivated the earth. In biblical times, the Hebrews celebrated the Feast of the Tabernacles, and a bit later, the Greeks put on an annual party to honor Demeter, the goddess of the harvest. The Romans feted Ceres, the goddess of grain, in a holiday called Cerealia (General Mills take note). In the Middle Ages the French celebrated the Feast of St. Martin of Tours as Martinmas, which featured a gala goose dinner.

The Pilgrims' three-day festival in 1621 is credited by most as the beginning of what Americans know as Thanksgiving. The celebration was proclaimed by Governor William Bradford to commemorate the survival of the colony through its first difficult year. Of the original 102 settlers who arrived at Plymouth in the winter of 1620, only 55 were still alive by the spring of 1621.

Perhaps the entire colony would have perished were it not for the help of the Wampanoag Indians, who taught the colonists how to hunt and fish, as well as how to cultivate corn and other native vegetables. These American crops kept the Pilgrims alive.

The feast of celebration featured venison, game birds (including wild turkeys, we hope), and the bounty of the fields, including pumpkins, squash, and corn. There were games, displays of arms, and general good will between the colonists and the Indians.

Over the next 200 years occasional national days of thanksgiving were celebrated for specific events, such as a victory over the British or the end of the War of 1812. Individual states instituted regular observances, but

there was no regular national Thanksgiving holiday until Sarah Josepha Hale, the author of "Mary Had a Little Lamb" and editor of *Godey's Lady's Book,* an influential magazine, began a movement to have the last Thursday in November established as the permanent day of celebration.

From 1846 until 1863 Mrs. Hale relentlessly lobbied for the holiday. She not only saw it as a patriotic day but also as a day for families and friends. She devoted the November issue of her magazine to the subject, she wrote to congressmen and governors, and she petitioned the president. Finally, on October 3, 1863, President Abraham Lincoln declared Thanksgiving Day a national holiday.

Feasting became a national pastime. The holiday also became a focus for parades and football games. The first big parade was the 1921 Gimbel's procession in Philadelphia, and professional football has been an obsession for decades.

After President Franklin Roosevelt tried to change the date to two weeks earlier to encourage a longer Christmas shopping season, Congress passed a law in 1941 that permanently fixed the date as the fourth Thursday in November.

Thanksgiving Dinner

Planning Ahead

The Thanksgiving dinner requires planning. Each dish must be selected and a shopping list written. Think well in advance about place settings, flowers, wines, tables, chairs, serving dishes, timing, and the guest list. It is important to get started early. Don't wait until the day before or even the week before. Thanksgiving is not a potluck dinner; it is a complex feast that requires organization and considerable precision.

We think about Thanksgiving all year long—discussing and planning, fine tuning the combination of flavors, textures, and colors. But we are obsessed. Normal people need to give the holiday feast some thought by the first of November.

At that time, sit down for a few minutes and sketch out the Thanksgiving meal. Keeping in mind the number of people you expect and who they are, tailor a balanced and appropriate menu.

Become a list maker. Make a list of guests. Make a list of things to do. Make a shopping list. Make a schedule for the days leading up to Thanksgiving.

By the second week of November you should have bought all your staples. Such nonperishables as flour, baking powder, canned goods, onions, potatoes, paper products, wines, spices, and any extra utensils, pans, and dishes should be purchased that week and kept separate from your day-to-day kitchen items. We like to keep the Thanksgiving provisions together in boxes. This way, when it's time to start preparations, everything is already together. Shopping early helps to avoid the last-minute crisis of finding a key item already sold out at your market. It also helps you to bypass the long, slow lines that always develop during the week before Thanksgiving.

Also by the end of the second week of November you should have ordered your fresh turkey. Arrange to pick it up on the Wednesday before Thanksgiving to minimize the time it has to spend in the home refrigerator. If you can reserve other important items—sweet potatoes, Brussels sprouts, persimmons, and so on—do it. Try to avoid as many surprises as possible.

INGREDIENTS

When you shop, here are a few pointers about the ingredients required for the recipes in this book:

BUTTER   We always use unsalted butter. If you use salted butter be sure to reduce the salt in the recipes accordingly. Unsalted is more perishable than salted butter, but it will keep for weeks in the freezer.

FLOUR   We generally use unbleached all-purpose flour.

EGGS   We use large eggs. If you have medium eggs, adjust the recipe by dividing the number of eggs by ¾. This means a recipe that calls for 3 eggs should be changed to 4 eggs.

DRIED HERBS AND SPICES   Most of us keep dried herbs and spices around too long. They lose their potency after six months to a year on the shelf. Unfortunately, most spice companies do not make it easy to determine how old their products are. When in doubt, throw it out. Why let a little tin or jar of lifeless herbs or spices spoil a great dish?

YIELDS

Most of the recipes in this book are for a party of twelve, a typical number for a family Thanksgiving dinner. Using twelve as a basic unit, we like to modularize the holiday feast. We don't feel it is necessary to vary the size of most dishes—other than the turkey—to accommodate a smaller or larger party. Instead, the dinner can be diminished or enlarged by subtracting or adding dishes.

Let us give examples of this kind of planning:

APPETIZERS

Gravlax

Ojai Valley Carrot Soup

MAIN MEAL

12-pound Turkey with Molasses Glaze

Our Favorite Gravy with (or Without) Giblets

Sausage-Crouton Stuffing

Cranberry Chutney

Winter White Purée · Baby Beets with Ginger Glaze

The Ultimate Mashed Potatoes

DESSERTS

Our Favorite Pumpkin Pie

Chocolate-Chestnut Mousse

Philadelphia Vanilla Ice Cream

Thanksgiving Dinner

APPETIZERS

Gravlax

Chicken Liver Mousse with Apple and Walnuts

Ojai Valley Carrot Soup

MAIN MEAL

18-pound Turkey with Molasses Glaze

Our Favorite Gravy with (or Without) Giblets

Sausage-Crouton Stuffing

Cranberry Chutney · Meems' Prune Chutney

Baby Beets with Ginger Glaze

Golden Winter Purée · Winter White Purée

Brussels Sprouts with Maple-Mustard Sauce

The Ultimate Mashed Potatoes

DESSERTS

Our Favorite Pumpkin Pie · Pear Mincemeat Pie

Ginger-Applesauce Spice Cake with Ginger Whipped Cream

Chocolate-Chestnut Mousse

Philadelphia Vanilla Ice Cream

APPETIZERS

Cheddar Cheese Crisps

Gravlax · Tuna Pâté

Chicken Liver Mousse with Apple and Walnuts

Ojai Valley Carrot Soup

MAIN MEAL

Two 15-pound Turkeys with Molasses Glaze

Our Favorite Gravy with (or Without) Giblets

Sausage-Crouton Stuffing · Pistachio and Apple Stuffing

Kumquat Cranberry Compote

Cranberry Chutney · Meems' Prune Chutney

Baby Beets with Ginger Glaze

Garlic, Spinach, and Rice Casserole

Golden Winter Purée · Winter White Purée

Schatze's Corn Pudding

Brussels Sprouts with Maple-Mustard Sauce

The Ultimate Mashed Potatoes

Buttermilk-Sage Biscuits

DESSERTS

Our Favorite Pumpkin Pie · Pear Mincemeat Pie · Apple Pie

Pumpkin-Ginger Cheesecake

Ginger-Applesauce Spice Cake with Ginger Whipped Cream

Chocolate-Chestnut Mousse

Philadelphia Vanilla Ice Cream

Thanksgiving Dinner

As the number of dishes increases, people take a smaller amount of each. For this reason you will see that some recipes show a range of servings. For pies, for example, we have put "Serves 8 to 12." Under normal circumstances, when the pie is the only dessert, cutting it into 8 pieces is proper. When there are four or five different desserts available, smaller servings are much more in order.

Offering a selection of desserts or vegetables also gets people to make choices. Guests at our house decide to take only three or four out of seven vegetables, for instance.

If you choose not to use this modular method, you can make fewer dishes, increasing the amount. Most of the recipes in the book can be doubled easily (or halved, for that matter).

ADVANCE PREPARATION

With very few exceptions, the recipes in this book can be done ahead of time. Most Thanksgiving cooks have at one time or another in their careers learned the cruel lesson that there is nothing more depressing than slaving away in the kitchen while your guests are in the living room enjoying themselves.

Thanksgiving is a family holiday and it should be enjoyed by all— including those who are charged with getting the food on the table.

With this in mind, we have put together a group of recipes that can be made anywhere from Thanksgiving morning to two months before. The few dishes that require last-minute attention are more appropriate for smaller, less pressurized gatherings.

Appetizers and Soups

*A*t our house, we don't worry too much about Thanksgiving appetizers. It doesn't make a great deal of sense to us to spend lots of time on a first course when the dinner that follows it is so ample.

Generally, we like to serve finger foods—spiced nuts, crunchy crisps, and an occasional pâté—things that people can serve for themselves. When you are basting the turkey, warming plates, and finishing the meal, there is no time to serve a fussy appetizer.

Before dinner, we encourage our guests and family to assemble in the living room, where we place dishes and bowls of appetizers to keep them busy. Eventually, everyone drifts into the kitchen.

Our kitchen is big and airy, the focus of our home. When we bought the house twelve years ago, we took out the ancient kitchen and dingy pantries and opened up the whole space. We knew that most of our family moments and all of our parties would take place there. So we designed a room with a central island and lots of space.

At Thanksgiving, when everyone congregates in the kitchen before the meal, we like to serve soup in glass mugs. While the turkey is being carved, everyone stands around sipping and talking. When they finally do sit down, turkey and all the trimmings await them.

Cheddar Cheese Crisps

*I*t isn't easy finding a good before-dinner munch that is both easy to prepare and not filling. These crackers are simple, quick, and not perishable. You can serve them warm or at room temperature. They can be made well ahead of time and then briefly warmed in a low oven.

Makes about 60 crackers

3 cups all-purpose flour
1½ cups chilled shortening
1 teaspoon salt
¾ cup finely grated sharp
   cheddar cheese

1 egg
1 tablespoon cider vinegar
2 tablespoons ice water

1. In a bowl, mix until crumbly the flour, shortening, salt and ¼ cup of the cheese. In another bowl, beat the egg, vinegar, and water.

2. Combine the flour and egg mixtures, and knead until the dough forms a ball. (This procedure can be done in the work bowl of a food processor fitted with the plastic dough blade. Pulse two or three times; do not overmix.) Wrap in wax paper and refrigerate overnight.

3. Preheat the oven to 350 degrees. Roll the dough out ⅛ inch thick. Cut into 2-inch rounds. (Ovals or rectangles would also be appropriate. In fact, a mixture of shapes is an interesting way to serve these.) Place on a cookie sheet lined with foil. Gather up the scraps, roll out again and cut more crackers.

4. Bake for 8 minutes. Top each cracker with a generous pinch of grated cheese. Bake for 10 to 12 more minutes, or until the cheese is melted and golden brown. Let cool for at least a few minutes before serving.

ADVANCE PREPARATION: Can be prepared 3 days in advance. Store in a covered tin in a cool place. Warm in a 300-degree oven before serving.

Schatze's Cheese Crackers

*A*ndy's mother, affectionately known as Schatze (pronounced Shot-zee), is a talented cook. She makes these crackers for her bridge group, for cocktail parties, and on Thanksgiving. They are always a big hit with guests before dinner.

Makes about 65 crackers

1½ cups grated sharp cheddar cheese
1 cup all-purpose flour
½ teaspoon salt
¼ teaspoon cayenne
8 tablespoons (1 stick) unsalted butter, frozen and cut into pieces

1 teaspoon Worcestershire sauce
1 egg yolk, lightly beaten
Assorted toppings: carraway seeds, poppy seeds, sesame seeds, slivered almonds, curry powder, various seasoning mixes

1. Place the cheese, flour, salt, cayenne, butter, and Worcestershire sauce in the bowl of a food processor fitted with a metal blade. Pulse several times until the mixture forms a ball. Remove from the processor and knead on a lightly floured surface by pushing forward with the heel of your hand 6 or 8 times. Divide the dough in half. Wrap the dough in wax paper and refrigerate for 3 hours or overnight.

2. Preheat the oven to 350 degrees. On a well-floured surface, roll out each ball of dough about ⅛ inch thick. Cut into rounds with a cookie cutter, or into squares or triangles with a pizza cutter (one with a fluted edge makes an attractive cracker).

3. Paint the top of each cracker with egg yolk. Top each cracker with one or more of the suggested toppings.

4. Place on a foil-lined cookie sheet, and bake 12 minutes or until golden brown. Cool on paper towels.

ADVANCE PREPARATION: Can be prepared 3 days ahead. Store in a covered tin in the refrigerator. They also can be frozen for several weeks. When ready to serve, warm in a 300-degree oven for 15 minutes.

Herb Crisps

$\mathcal{T}$hese are really simple and very delicious. No matter how many you make, there are never any left.

Makes about 30

1 cup all-purpose flour
1 tablespoon finely minced garlic
1 teaspoon ground cumin
1 teaspoon onion salt
1 teaspoon celery seed
½ teaspoon cayenne
½ teaspoon superfine sugar
8 tablespoons (1 stick) chilled
  unsalted butter, cut into
  pieces

2 tablespoons plus about 1
  teaspoon ice water
1 large egg white, lightly beaten
3 teaspoons herbes de Provence,
  or a mixture of dried thyme,
  basil, savory, and fennel seed

1. Mix the flour, garlic, cumin, onion salt, celery seed, cayenne, and sugar in a medium bowl. Add the butter and cut in until the mixture resembles fine meal. Gradually mix in enough ice water to form a dough that just comes together. Do not overmix. Divide the dough in half; flatten each half into a rectangle. Wrap each piece in plastic wrap and refrigerate for 1 hour.

2. Preheat the oven to 350 degrees. On a lightly floured surface, roll 1 piece of dough at a time to form a thick rectangle 5 inches by ¾ inches by ¼ inch thick. Cut the dough crosswise into ¾-inch strips. Place the strips on an ungreased cookie sheet, spacing evenly. Brush each one with egg white, being careful not to let any drip onto the baking sheet.

3. Sprinkle half the herb mixture over the dough strips. Refrigerate for 15 minutes. Bake for 20 minutes or until puffed and crisp. Transfer to a rack. Repeat with the remaining dough, egg white, and herbs.

ADVANCE PREPARATION: Can be prepared up to 3 days in advance. Cool and store between sheets of wax paper in an airtight container at room temperature. Serve warm or at room temperature.

Spiced Almonds

Makes 3 cups

¾ pound whole blanched almonds
2 tablespoons vegetable oil
2 tablespoons Cointreau
1 tablespoon unsalted butter, melted
¼ cup sugar

1 teaspoon vanilla extract
2 teaspoons ground cinnamon
½ teaspoon freshly grated nutmeg
½ teaspoon ground cloves
Salt

1. In a bowl, whisk together the oil, Cointreau, butter, and sugar. Marinate the nuts in the mixture for 15 minutes.

2. Preheat the oven to 350 degrees. Spread nuts in a single layer on a baking sheet lined with foil. Toast in preheated oven for 25 minutes or until golden.

3. In a bowl, mix the vanilla, cinnamon, nutmeg, and cloves. Toss hot nuts in the spice mixture to coat. Sprinkle with salt. Spread the nuts on paper towels and cool completely.

ADVANCE PREPARATION: These will benefit from being prepared at least 2 days ahead. Store in an airtight tin at room temperature.

Spiced Macadamia Nuts

$\mathcal{T}$hese are impossible to resist and don't require much time at all to make. We have settled on cooking them in a wok because it heats oil quickly and makes stirring easy.

Makes 2 cups

12 ounces whole macadamia nuts	½ teaspoon freshly grated nutmeg
⅔ cup sugar	½ teaspoon ground mace
¼ cup water	¼ teaspoon ground cloves
1 whole vanilla bean, split	1 cup vegetable oil
2 teaspoons ground cinnamon	Salt

1. Spray or brush a baking sheet with cooking oil and set aside.

2. In a small saucepan, bring 2 cups of water to a boil. Add the nuts and cook 1 minute. Strain and turn out on paper towels to dry.

3. In the same saucepan combine sugar and water. Over medium heat, stir to dissolve, brushing any sugar crystals away from the sides of the saucepan with a pastry brush dipped in water. Swirl to melt any crystals while continuing to boil until the sugar forms a thick syrup (248 degrees on a candy thermometer or soft-ball stage). Add the seeds from the vanilla bean and all the spices and stir to combine.

4. In a wok, heat the oil to 375 degrees. It will smoke slightly.

5. Add about one-third of the nuts to the spicy sugar mixture and coat thoroughly. Working quickly, remove the nuts with a slotted spoon, drain off as much sugar syrup as possible, and put the nuts into the hot oil. Stir-fry until they are a mahogany color, about 10 to 15 seconds. Remove from the oil, using the slotted spoon, and place on the greased baking sheet. Separate the nuts with tongs. Repeat until all the nuts are cooked. Salt to taste.

SERVING SUGGESTION: These nuts can be served warm or at room temperature. Other nuts—almonds, walnuts, pecans, or cashews—can be substituted, but mixed nuts are not a good idea. Nuts have such a variety of cooking temperatures that some will burn while others won't be done.

ADVANCE PREPARATION: These will benefit from being prepared at least 2 days ahead. Store in an airtight tin at room temperature.

Spiced Mixed Nuts

Makes 3 cups

1 pound roasted, unsalted mixed nuts	1 tablespoon sugar
2 egg whites	1 tablespoon salt
8 tablespoons (1 stick) unsalted butter, melted	1 tablespoon ground cinnamon
¼ cup Amaretto	1 teaspoon ground mace
	1 teaspoon ground ginger

1. Blanch the nuts by putting them into boiling water and counting 10 seconds after the water returns to a boil. Strain and turn them onto a baking sheet to cool.

2. Preheat the oven to 325 degrees. In a bowl gently beat the egg white until foamy and then add the remaining ingredients. Mix to combine. Add the nuts and stir until coated. Spread the nuts in one layer on the baking sheet lined with foil. Bake them in the preheated oven for 20 minutes, tossing them two or three times during the cooking.

3. Cool the nuts to room temperature before serving.

ADVANCE PREPARATION: These will benefit from being prepared at least 2 days ahead. Store in an airtight tin at room temperature.

Pacbag Tuna Pâté

One of our favorite San Francisco restaurants is the Pacific Heights Bar and Grill or, as it is affectionately known by its regulars, the Pacbag. This recipe of Chef Ellis Casabar has recently become a regular appetizer in our house and it works very nicely as a warm-up to the holiday feast. To heighten its festive appearance, garnish the pâté with extra chopped pistachios, and dress up the crock with an arrangement of seasonal fruits. Serve with rye toast points or toasted rounds of French bread.

This recipe makes enough for a good-sized cocktail party and more than enough for a preamble to a big dinner. You can halve the recipe easily, or leave it as is and eat the extra during the holiday weekend.

Makes 5 cups

1 pound tuna fillet (use ahi, if
    you can get it), poached (see
    below) and cooled
¾ cup Cognac or brandy
1 tablespoon freshly ground
    pepper

½ cup chopped fresh dill
1 pound cream cheese
4 hard-boiled eggs, peeled and
    chopped
¾ cup chopped pistachio nuts
Salt

1. In the bowl of a food processor fitted with the metal blade, place the tuna, Cognac, pepper, and dill. Process for 15 seconds or until smooth. Add the cream cheese and eggs. Pulse 3 to 4 times to blend.

2. Pour into a terrine or crock. Line the crock with parchment paper. Fold in the pistachios and salt to taste. Chill well before serving.

Court Bouillon

Makes 3¼ cups

3 cups water
¼ cup dry white wine
1 tablespoon lemon juice

1 bay leaf
5 whole peppercorns

In a 3-quart saucepan, combine all the ingredients and bring to a boil. Add the fish. Let the liquid come back to a boil, but turn the heat down so the water just barely simmers. Cover and cook until the fish is just done, about 10 minutes. Don't overcook or the fish will be dry.

ADVANCE PREPARATION: Can be prepared 1 day ahead. Cover and refrigerate.

Gravlax

*T*his Swedish method for marinating fresh salmon at home was certainly not served at the first Thanksgiving, but we find it to be a perfect appetizer. We start marinating on Monday and by Thursday we have a delicious and easy-to-serve warm-up for the big dinner.

Serves 12 or more

3½ pounds fresh salmon fillet,
   cleaned and scaled, center
   cut, skin on
1 large bunch fresh dill

⅓ cup coarse salt
⅓ cup sugar
2 tablespoons white
   peppercorns, crushed

1. Examine the fish carefully for bones and use tweezers to remove those that remain.

2. Place half of the fish, skin side down, in a high-sided glass or enamel baking dish that fits it snugly. Chop the dill coarsely and spread it over the fish. Mix the salt, sugar, and peppercorns, and sprinkle them evenly over the fish. Top with the other half of the fish, skin side up.

3. Cover the dish with heavy-duty foil. Try to find a plate, a board, or something else that fits inside the edges of the dish. Then weight down the board with heavy cans, books, or rocks. (We use a foil-wrapped brick.)

4. Refrigerate. Turn the fish over every 12 hours, spooning the liquid in the dish between the two sections of fish each time you do. Continue this procedure for at least 48 hours and preferably for 72 hours.

5. When you are ready to serve the gravlax, remove the fish from the dish. Scrape away the dill and remaining marinade and pat dry with paper towels.

6. Slice the salmon across the grain with a sharp, straight knife, detaching each slice from the skin as you cut. Serve on thin slices of pumpernickel with mustard dill sauce.

Mustard Dill Sauce

Makes 1½ cups

½ cup dark English mustard
1 tablespoon dry mustard
6 tablespoons sugar

¼ cup white wine vinegar
⅔ cup olive oil
6 tablespoons finely minced dill

1. In a medium bowl, mix the mustards, sugar, and vinegar into a smooth paste.

2. Whisk in the olive oil, drop by drop, until the sauce begins to thicken. Continue whisking while pouring the oil in a thin stream. The sauce should be like mayonnaise. Stir in the dill. Refrigerate until ready to use. Whisk again just before using.

ADVANCE PREPARATION: The gravlax requires three days preparation and it will keep in the refrigerator for a week after being cured. The sauce can be prepared 3 days ahead. It will keep in the refrigerator for a week. However, if making the sauce in advance, omit the chopped dill and add just before serving.

Chicken Liver Mousse with Apple and Walnuts

*T*his smooth appetizer will keep the hungry hordes at bay until you are ready to serve the turkey. It is based on an idea by Diane Rossen Worthington.

Makes 5 cups

1 cup walnuts, broken into small pieces
5 tablespoons unsalted butter
1 medium onion, finely chopped
3 shallots, minced
2 tart green apples such as Pippin or Granny Smith, cored, peeled, and minced
2 cloves garlic, minced
¼ pound chicken-apple sausage, or any mild sausage
1 pound chicken livers

½ cup Calvados
10 ounces cream cheese, at room temperature, cut into chunks
1 tablespoon chopped fresh tarragon, or 1 teaspoon dried
1½ tablespoons chopped fresh thyme, or 1½ teaspoon dried
1½ teaspoons freshly ground white pepper
1 teaspoon salt

1. Roast the walnuts on a cookie sheet lined with foil in a 350-degree oven for 7 to 10 minutes. Set aside.

2. In a skillet over medium heat, melt 3 tablespoons of butter. Add the onion, shallots, and apples, tossing to coat with butter. Sauté for 10 minutes or until translucent. Add the garlic and sauté about 1 minute. Set aside and cool slightly.

3. Place another skillet over medium heat. Melt 2 tablespoons of butter, and sauté the sausage meat removed from the casing. After about 2 minutes add the chicken livers and sear on each side. Continue cooking for 3 minutes. The chicken livers should be pink inside. Add Calvados, ignite (being careful to avert your eyes), and set aside to cool.

4. Place the onion and apple mixture in the bowl of a food processor fitted with the metal blade. Pulse until the mixture is pastelike but not smooth. Add the cream cheese and process for about 10 seconds. Add the chicken liver mixture and the seasonings. Process to combine, occasionally stopping to scrape down the sides. Add the walnuts, and pulse two or three times, just to incorporate.

5. Put the mixture in a 5- or 6-cup terrine or crock.

VARIATION: Replace half the sausage with ⅛ pound spicy duck sausage, and sauté the two together in step 3. Add ½ teaspoon red pepper flakes with the other seasonings.

SERVING SUGGESTIONS: Remove from the refrigerator about 2 hours before serving to bring to room temperature. Serve with crackers, toast, or slivers of celery.

ADVANCE PREPARATION: Can be prepared 1 day ahead. Cover and refrigerate. Bring to room temperature before serving. Will keep for 3 days. Can also be frozen for up to 2 months.

Yam Soup

The great charm of this thick soup is that it presents the lush, rich flavor of yams with only slight adornment. If you find yams too waxy as a vegetable, you might prefer them as a soup.

Serves 12

6 yams (about 3 pounds)
8 cups Chicken Stock (see page 77)
2 cups heavy cream
½ teaspoon freshly grated nutmeg
¼ teaspoon ground cinnamon
¼ teaspoon ground mace

2 tablespoons lemon juice
½ teaspoon freshly ground white pepper
Salt
Crème fraîche or sour cream (optional)

1. Peel the yams and cut them into 1-inch pieces. Place in a saucepan and cover with the chicken broth. Bring to a boil, cover, and simmer for 45 minutes. Pour into a food processor or food mill and purée.

2. Return the purée to the saucepan and stir in all the other ingredients. Bring to a simmer over moderate heat and serve immediately. If desired, top each serving with a dollop of crème fraîche or sour cream.

ADVANCE PREPARATION: Can be prepared 2 days in advance. Cover and refrigerate.

Turkey Consommé

This clear soup is elegant yet loaded with flavor. It is a perfect starter for a Thanksgiving party where the main course is something other than turkey. Try the optional dumplings; they add a festive dimension. You can freeze what you don't serve. It will keep 3 months.

Makes 1 gallon

12 egg whites
6 egg shells
1½ cups coarsely chopped celery
1 cup coarsely chopped leeks, whites only
½ cup coarsely chopped onion
½ cup peeled and coarsely chopped carrots
Handful of parsley stems

1 pound ground uncooked turkey
1 teaspoon whole allspice berries
1 teaspoon black peppercorns
1 teaspoon salt
3 quarts poultry stock, at room temperature (see pages 77, 78)

1. In the bowl of a food processor fitted with the metal blade, place all the ingredients except the stock. Pulse to combine.

2. Put the stock in a large pot. Pour in the mixture from the food processor. Stir to mix. Heat slowly, stirring constantly, until the consommé reaches 168 degrees on a thermometer. Stop stirring. A coagulated mass called a *raft* will form. Let the stock come to a boil. Reduce the heat immediately, allowing the stock to simmer. This gentle bubbling action will clarify the stock into a consommé. Check the pot frequently to make sure the stock does not boil violently. This process should take about 1 hour.

3. Turn off the heat. Allow the consommé to cool and the raft to solidify. The challenge is removing the raft and keeping the consommé clear. Using a slotted spoon scoop up spoonfuls of the raft and discard. If the soup didn't clarify, this process can be repeated.

4. To remove any traces of the raft, pass the consommé through thoroughly rinsed cheesecloth. Reheat prior to serving.

SERVING SUGGESTION: The beauty of a consommé is its versatility. A fine dice of vegetables or dumplings adds interest to the soup. Try these almond quenelles.

Creamy Almond Quenelles

Makes about 24 dumplings

1 cup bread crumbs
¼ cup all-purpose flour
2 eggs
2 tablespoons unsalted butter,
    melted

¼ cup ground almonds
Few drops almond extract

1. Combine all ingredients in a food processor fitted with a metal blade. Pulse to blend. The dough should be light and fluffy.

2. In a 1-quart saucepan, bring 2 cups of stock or consommé to a boil, reduce to a simmer. Using two spoons, form quenelles and slide them into the simmering liquid. The quenelles are done when they float to the top and resist a slight pressure when touched. They take about 2 minutes to cook. Serve two in each bowl

ADVANCE PREPARATION: The consommé can be prepared 2 days ahead. Cover and refrigerate. It will keep in the freezer for several months. The quenelles can be made 1 day ahead. Cover and refrigerate. Reheat in the hot soup.

Ojai Valley Carrot Soup

*T*his soup may never have been served in the Ojai Valley, a spectacular spot near Santa Barbara, California. Our son Toby was graduated from the Thacher School in Ojai and while we were there for the ceremony, we conceived this recipe.

Makes 8 cups

SOUP

4 leeks, whites only
2 pounds carrots, peeled, tops removed
3 tablespoons olive oil
¼ cup Arborio rice
3 cups Chicken Stock, fresh (see page 77) or canned

1 tablespoon minced crystallized ginger
½ teaspoon sea salt
½ teaspoon freshly ground pepper
¼ cup freshly squeezed lime juice

GARNISH

2 tablespoons crème fraîche
2 tablespoons lime zest

1 tablespoon minced crystallized ginger

1. Slice the leeks lengthwise, then slice into thin half-moon shapes. Cut the carrots into 2-inch lengths.

2. In a stock pot, heat the oil and sauté the leeks until soft. Add the carrots, rice, and stock. Bring to a boil, then simmer for 40 minutes. Add the ginger. Cook for an additional 10 minutes.

3. Purée the mixture in batches in a blender or food processor fitted with a metal blade. Put the purée through the food processor power strainer, if available. Return the soup to the pot and season with salt and pepper.

4. Add the lime juice, thoroughly combining it with the soup. Serve warm with a dollop of crème fraîche and a sprinkling of lime zest and crystallized ginger.

ADVANCE PREPARATION: The soup can be prepared 2 days in advance. Cover and refrigerate. Reheat before serving.

Chestnut Soup

*T*his is one of the best things we've ever tasted. The two pounds of whole roasted chestnuts are the only problem. If you use the excellent jarred versions imported from France (we use Minerve brand), the cost can be high. If you roast and peel them yourself, the time and effort is substantial. Nevertheless, this is such a delicious soup, it's worth it either way.

Serves 6

8 tablespoons (1 stick) unsalted butter	½ cup Madeira
2 pounds roasted and peeled chestnuts	2 fresh parsley sprigs
1 carrot, peeled and sliced	Pinch of freshly grated nutmeg
1 parsnip, peeled and sliced	½ teaspoon salt
1 cup peeled and chopped celery root	½ teaspoon freshly ground pepper
7½ cups Chicken Stock (see page 77)	Crème fraîche, sour cream, or plain yogurt
	Cayenne
	2 tablespoons chopped parsley

1. Melt half the butter over medium heat in a large heavy skillet. Add the chestnuts and sauté until heated through, about 5 minutes. Set aside.

2. Melt the remaining butter in a large heavy pot over medium heat. Add the carrot, parsnip, and celery root, and sauté until soft, about 7 minutes.

3. Add the stock to the vegetables and bring to a boil. Reduce heat to low. Add the chestnuts, Madeira, parsley, nutmeg, salt, and pepper. Simmer for 15 minutes.

4. Ladle one-third of the mixture into the work bowl of a food processor fitted with the metal blade. Process for 30 seconds. Pour into a bowl or another stockpot. Repeat this procedure until all the soup has been processed to a smooth texture. (If you want a few small nuggets of chestnut in the final product, cut down on the processing time of the last batch.)

5. Return the soup to a simmer, stirring frequently. Adjust seasoning. Ladle into bowls. Top each with a dollop of crème fraîche, sour cream, or yogurt. Sprinkle with cayenne and chopped parsley.

ADVANCE PREPARATION: Can be prepared up to 2 days ahead. Cover and refrigerate.

Cream of Jerusalem Artichoke Soup

*J*erusalem artichokes are not artichokes at all; they are the tubers of sunflowers. They are also known as *sunchokes* and *girasole.* We love their flavor and this soup is an excellent showcase for this lovely and slightly exotic vegetable.

Serves 12

3 pounds Jerusalem artichokes
8 tablespoons (1 stick) unsalted
   butter
3 large onions, thinly sliced
3 cloves garlic, minced
12 cups Chicken Stock (see page
   77)

2 cups heavy cream
Salt and freshly ground white
   pepper
4 tablespoons minced fresh
   parsley
Paprika

1. Wash the Jerusalem artichokes thoroughly. Clean them with a brush under running water. Cut them into chunks.

2. Melt the butter in a 5-quart saucepan. Sauté the artichokes, onions, and garlic for 5 minutes, or until soft. Add the stock and simmer for 45 minutes.

3. Process the soup in a food processor fitted with the metal blade, or pass it through a food mill. Return the purée to the saucepan. Stir in the cream. Season to taste. Garnish each serving with a sprinkling of parsley and paprika.

ADVANCE PREPARATION: Can be prepared 2 days in advance. Cover and refrigerate.

Roasted Butternut Squash
and Garlic Soup

Serves 6

1 butternut squash (approximately 2 pounds)	2½ cups Chicken Stock (see page 77)
3 tablespoons olive oil	1 teaspoon freshly ground white pepper
1 head garlic, cloves unpeeled	1 teaspoon salt
1 cup hot water	

1. Preheat the oven to 350 degrees. Slice the squash in half lengthwise, and remove the seeds and stringy pulp with a spoon. Rub the flat side with olive oil and place the squash, cut side down, in a glass baking dish; sprinkle the garlic cloves around the squash. Add the water and the rest of the oil. Bake for 1 to 1½ hours, or until the squash is very soft. Remove from the oven and cool slightly.

2. Scoop the squash pulp into the bowl of a food processor fitted with the metal blade. Squeeze the pointed end of each garlic clove, letting its pulp drop into the food processor.

3. Process for 30 seconds, until the mixture is very smooth. Add the chicken stock ½ cup at a time, pulsing the processor after each addition. Add the pepper and salt. Pour the mixture into a 2-quart saucepan and place over medium heat. Bring to a simmer and adjust the seasonings.

VARIATION: Add ¼ cup orange juice with the chicken stock and 1 tablespoon curry powder with the seasonings.

ADVANCE PREPARATION: Can be prepared 2 days in advance. Cover and refrigerate.

Thanksgiving Dinner

L 'Avenue is one of the most innovative new restaurants in San Francisco. This is L'Avenue's Chef Nancy Oakes's version of harvest vegetable soup. It is loaded with flavor and texture, and it has a surprising flash of peppery heat on the palate.

Serves 12

1 medium yellow onion, diced
3 cloves garlic, chopped
3 large leeks, white part only, diced
2 carrots, peeled and diced
3 celery stalks, diced
3 tablespoons virgin olive oil
1 medium perfection squash or 2 acorn squash, peeled and diced
3 zucchini, diced
1 butternut squash, peeled and cubed
2 jalapeno peppers, seeded and diced

1 red bell pepper, diced
Salt and freshly ground pepper
5½ cups good rich Chicken or Turkey stock (see pages 77, 78)
8 small acorn squash (for presentation)
1 cup heavy cream
1 teaspoon fresh (or ½ teaspoon dried) thyme, chopped
3 tablespoons finely diced candied ginger
3 tablespoons finely chopped toasted hazelnuts
Crème fraîche

1. In a large skillet, sauté the onion, garlic, leeks, carrots, and celery in the olive oil until soft. Add all the squash, zucchini, and the peppers. Sauté until blended with the other ingredients. Season to taste and add the chicken stock. Simmer over medium heat until the squash is soft, about 10 minutes.

2. Purée the soup with a blender, food mill, or food processor. Remove 2 cups of the purée and set aside. Pass the remainder through a fine sieve or the power strainer of the food processor. Return the reserved 2 cups to the soup.

3. Preheat the oven to 350 degrees. Cut the tops off the 8 small acorn squash. Scoop out their seeds. Oil their skins and season the inside with salt and pepper. Turn the squash upside down on a baking sheet and bake about 20 minutes in the preheated oven, or until a fork pierces the inner squash meat easily.

4. Flatten the bottom of the squash so that it will sit firmly on a plate. Make sure the shells are intact.

5. Add the cream and thyme to the soup and reheat but do not boil. Add the ginger and hazelnuts. Ladle the hot soup into the prepared squash shells, placing a dollop of crème fraîche in each. Serve.

If you want to forgo using the squash as soup bowls, just skip steps 3 and 4 and go to step 5, using soup bowls.

ADVANCE PREPARATION: Can be prepared 1 day ahead through step 2. Cover and refrigerate.

Celery Celery-Root Soup

S mooth and luscious with lovely, earthy harvest flavors, this soup is easy and quite elegant.

Serves 8

8 tablespoons (1 stick) butter
4 medium onions, thinly sliced
6 cups rich Chicken or Turkey
  Stock (see pages 77, 78)
4 medium celery root bulbs,
  peeled and diced (6 cups)
1 head celery, cleaned, scraped
  of strings, and diced

2 cups heavy cream or milk (for
  a lighter version)
Salt and freshly ground white
  pepper
1 tart apple, peeled, cut into
  ¼-inch dice, sautéed in 1
  tablespoon butter (optional)

1. Melt the butter in a 4-quart saucepan over medium heat. Sauté the onions in the butter until translucent. Add chicken stock. Add the celery root and celery. Simmer over medium heat until the vegetables are tender.

2. Purée the soup in batches in a food processor until it has a creamy texture. Run the puréed soup through a sieve to remove any lumps or fibers. Return to the pot and heat through. Season to taste. Add the cream or milk.

3. Sprinkle 1 tablespoon of diced apple on each serving.

ADVANCE PREPARATION: Can be prepared 2 days ahead. Cover and refrigerate. Warm over medium heat. Do not boil.

Turkey and Other Poultry

*T*he turkey has been a part of American culture since before the time of Columbus. Actually, this clumsy-looking bird—which some wrongly characterize as dumb—was roaming North America more than eight million years before man made his appearance. Domesticated turkeys were part of the diet of Southwestern Indians at the same time that Julius Caesar ruled Rome.

The value of the turkey as food was discovered immediately by Columbus and Cortez, who gathered up the birds and shipped them back to Europe. By 1530, turkeys were already being raised domestically in France, Italy, and England. Actually the first turkeys raised by the American colonists were not from the native populations, but rather from domesticated stock brought back from Europe. The European stock was crossed with the native wild turkey, and the resultant offspring were the forefathers and mothers of the Bronze turkey, the variety that became the basis of the American turkey industry.

The turkey is America's greatest contribution to the domesticated poultry industry. Benjamin Franklin himself declared the turkey to be the quintessential American avian. In fact, he proposed the turkey as the official United States bird, only to be deeply disappointed when the bald eagle got the nod instead. "I wish the bald eagle had not been chosen as the representative of our country!" he wrote to his daughter. "The turkey is a much more respectable bird, and withal a true original native of America."

The turkey got its name thanks to the same misconception that gave native Americans the title "Indians." Since Columbus thought the New World was connected to India, he assumed that the funny-looking birds were some form of peacock. He called them *tuka,* the Indian name for peacock. (Actually, the turkey is a variety of pheasant with the official scientific name of *Meleagris gallopavo.*)

The India mistake has carried over into some of the names given the bird in other languages. The French word is *dinde,* a contraction of *d'Inde,* meaning "of India," and the Dutch still persist in calling the turkey *calecutische hohn,* the "Calcutta hen."

The diet of early American settlers was dominated by game birds. The North American woodlands were filled with all sorts of delectable flying creatures, and colonists found them to be a ready source of food. The most populous species were passenger pigeons, which in the seventeenth century were estimated to be more than nine billion in number. Wholesale shooting and trapping of these birds brought them to extinction by the early twentieth century.

Luckily the same sad fate did not befall the turkey, which was also plentiful in the early American skies. The wild turkey was a common and noisy part of the natural environment when the first settlers arrived. Great flocks of them were reported in most mid-Atlantic states. In fact, by the 1820s wild turkeys were so common that they were actually disdained by gourmets. Farm chickens cost more. But European connoisseurs, who had been given less opportunity to become blasé about these tasty birds, raved about turkey from the beginning.

M. F. K. Fisher wrote about it in *Serve It Forth:* "French interest in anything from the American colonies ran high, and such dishes as Indian corn pudding and wild roasted turkey made any table smart. Prices for them ran into several figures—almost as expensive as truffles. It took a woman of unlimited income and capricious brain to combine the two whims of the moment, and serve a turkey stuffed with truffles to her admirers."

LOTS OF THEM, AND THEY'RE GOOD FOR YOU

Nearly 250 million turkeys are produced every year in the United States—one for every man, woman, and child in the country. The per capita consumption of turkey in the United States is more than 16 pounds per person, and this figure has been growing steadily since the beginning of the twentieth century. In 1930, per capita consumption was 1.5 pounds, in 1955 it was 5 pounds, in 1968 it was 8 pounds, and it was only 12 pounds as recently as 1985.

The trend toward lighter foods and a good promotional campaign by the National Turkey Federation, a grower association, have spurred consumers to eat turkey at other times besides Thanksgiving and Christmas. In 1987, for instance, only 40 percent of all turkeys consumed were eaten in the fourth quarter of the year.

The heaviest consumption of turkey takes place on the East and West Coasts. California has the highest rate of turkey consumption, averaging more than 23 pounds per person.

Turkey is low in calories and fat. Compared to other popular meats, it

can be considered diet food. Three ounces of pork loin contains 219 calories and 12.7 grams of fat. The same amount of roast beef has 217 calories and 12.9 grams of fat. Lamb chops yield 211 calories and 12.9 grams of fat. Dark turkey meat, on the other hand, has only 143 calories and 4.4 grams of fat, and turkey white meat, lowest of all, 119 calories and just 1 gram of fat. In general, turkey has fewer calories and less fat than chicken, too. Where the Thanksgiving feast becomes fattening is with side dishes—especially stuffing.

In addition to its dietetic charms, the turkey is also very economical. That same three ounces of pork loin mentioned above will cost $.71; the roast beef, $1.65; the lamb chops, $2.57; and even chicken rings in at $.43. Three ounces of turkey will cost only $.37 in 1990 dollars. One of the key reasons for this is the fact that turkey has an exceptionally high percentage of meat in relation to fat and bone. Turkey is 63 percent meat, while chicken is only 47 percent.

PRESENTING THE TURKEY OF THE NINETIES

Modern turkey farming has become a very scientific procedure. Thanks to turkey genetics, farmers are able to produce a pound of meat using a smaller amount of feed in less time than most other domestic meat-yielding animals require. Over the last 30 years or so, genetic scientists have also been able to develop a modern turkey that has a broad, thick breast, thicker thighs, plumper drumsticks, a higher meat-to-bone ratio, and white feathers. Although the turkey's original color was a mottled brown, growers prefer white because it leaves no unsightly pigment under the skin when the bird is plucked.

Today's turkey is raised on one of the more than 2,000 turkey farms in the United States. A typical farm raises 50,000 birds each year. Usually the turkeys are grown in barns that accommodate 7,000 toms (male turkeys) or 10,000 hens (females). In warmer climates the birds are raised outdoors on ranges that hold 5,000 to 10,000.

The turkey industry is completely entrepreneurial and receives no government support or subsidies. Birds are, however, carefully inspected for drug or pesticide residues by the USDA before they are processed. Turkeys are administered medication only when they contract minor diseases. They are not given hormones.

BREEDING IN THE MODERN WORLD

To meet the Thanksgiving demand, extra high quantities of eggs are incubated during April, May, and June. The egg takes 28 days to hatch. After that, a hen requires about 16 weeks to reach market weight and a tom about 19 weeks.

The modern, well-bred turkey is quite different from its wild ancestor. It is much more efficient at converting feed to protein (meat), it is heavier and more compact, and it grows to maturity much faster.

Most domesticated turkeys live on a healthy diet of corn and soybean meal mixed with a supplement of vitamins and minerals. They have a comfortable and pleasant life except for the sad fact that they are unable to mate naturally. Because of his sumo wrestler build, the modern tom turkey is physically incapable of performing his familial duties. As a result, hens are artificially inseminated, a procedure that increases the rate of fertility but certainly must have a negative impact on the turkey's quality of life.

When this problem first became apparent, growers tried all sorts of remedies. The difficulty was that the new-wave tom was too ungainly and clumsy to mount the hen and complete the necessary actions, so some growers devised canvas saddles that were placed on the hens. This helped only so long as the saddles didn't slip or get lost. When that happened the hens had to be caught and resaddled—quite a labor-intensive procedure.

But in the 1950s a technique was developed by Dr. Fred Lorenz and Dr. Frank Ogasawara for an artificial insemination technique that could be used on turkeys. This saved the turkey industry from a rather embarrassing situation and banished the poor, overstuffed tom, once and for all, from the hen coop.

KOSHER POULTRY

In most of the big cities of the United States, kosher turkeys and chickens are readily available. These birds are of high quality and have been raised in a hygienic environment.

Kosher is a very common word, but not that many people really know what it means. The laws of Kashruth are mostly found in the book of Deuteronomy in the Old Testament. They were given to protect the Jewish people from unclean food and to preserve the fair treatment of animals.

Here are the rules: There can be no mixing of meat with milk. Deuteronomy 14 states exactly which animals, poultry, and fish cannot be consumed. Animals without both cuds and cloven hoofs, fish without fins and scales, birds of prey, and insects and crustaceans—are all forbidden.

In addition, all permitted animals must be healthy, and ritually slaughtered and butchered according to a set of rules. Kosher does not refer to a type of food—it only has to do with the way food is treated and in what combinations it can be served.

Many non-Jews regularly buy their turkeys and other poultry from

kosher butchers. These products are of excellent quality and are generally indistinguishable in taste from those sold in better non-kosher shops.

EXPORTS

American turkeys are exported to a number of foreign countries. The biggest customer is Germany, with Venezuela, Japan, Hong Kong, Singapore, Egypt, Saudi Arabia, England, Holland, and Canada also buying significant amounts. The export business is good, but it could be much better except for the fact that some countries, through the use of high tariffs and excessively strict plant requirements, make it uneconomical for American producers to sell their products in some important foreign markets such as Great Britain and Brazil.

BUYING THE TURKEY

The modern turkey industry has made it easy to shop for turkey. The uniformity and high quality of the birds in the butcher shops and supermarkets mean there is really little need to be concerned about such things as freshness, tenderness, and flavor. Just buy from a reliable merchant and you should have no problems. This leaves several other important considerations, and the most important of these is size. How big a turkey should you buy?

Obviously, the size of your turkey is directly related to the number of people you will be feeding at Thanksgiving, but there are other factors that should also influence your choice. Do you want leftovers? Are your guests going to be mostly hungry adults or will there be a substantial number of children, who will eat smaller portions?

We like to estimate the size of the turkey needed by allotting 1 to 1½ pounds of uncooked meat for every person (allow 2 pounds per person if the turkey weighs less than 10 pounds). This leaves a good amount, and it also gives enough white and dark meat to satisfy our guests' preferences. Of course, this doesn't mean that you have to buy just one turkey. If we are having 30 people, instead of bringing home a husky 30-pound tom that will not fit in our oven, we buy two 15-pound birds and roast them side by side.

All turkeys today are classified as *young turkey.* A useful subcategory is *fryer-roaster,* usually a very young bird weighing 6 to 9 pounds and under 16 weeks of age. This size is excellent for a small group and for barbecuing outdoors (see page 48).

HANDLING

If you are selecting a frozen turkey, make sure it is wrapped in tight packaging that is completely free of holes and tears. Also be aware of expiration or "sell by" dates.

Take your fresh or frozen turkey home immediately after purchase and keep it frozen or refrigerated. If you are using a fresh turkey that is not enclosed in a tight plastic wrap, take it out of its wrappings and, after removing the bag containing the giblets, rinse it under cold, running water. Then pat it dry with paper towels, rewrap it in fresh wax paper and place it in a large, tightly sealed plastic bag in the refrigerator. Make the turkey the last thing you pick up before heading home so that it will not be left out of refrigeration for too long.

It is important that the turkey (and other foods) are handled in a clean environment. Make sure that utensils, platters, cutting boards, countertops, and hands are soap-and-hot-water clean. After handling fresh meats you should rinse your hands so as not to transfer bacteria to other foods

A fresh turkey—and any other uncooked meat, for that matter—should never be left unrefrigerated for more than 2 hours. The key temperatures to remember are 40 degrees and 140 degrees. If you are keeping the turkey (or any other perishable food) cold, it must be at 40 degrees or lower. If you are heating food, it must be 140 degrees or higher. The temperatures in between are ideal for the growth of bacteria and the production of toxins in food.

DEFROSTING

If you are using a frozen turkey, the best way to defrost it is in the refrigerator. This method is slow, but it results in a bird that loses very little of its moisture and will, therefore, cook up moist and tender.

Put the frozen turkey—still in its original wrap—on a platter or tray in the refrigerator. Allow 5 hours per pound of turkey for defrosting. This means that if you are preparing a 15-pound turkey, it will take 75 hours (3 days, 3 hours) to defrost. If you add the cooking time of 4 hours (5 hours stuffed) and 15 minutes resting time, you will know the exact time to start the defrosting procedure. In the case of the 15-pounder, if you want to serve the bird at 5:00 in the afternoon on Thursday, you will have to begin the defrosting at 9:00 A.M. on Monday.

If you need to defrost your turkey a little faster, place the still-wrapped bird in the sink on Wednesday morning and cover with cold water. Change the water frequently during the day and allow about 30 minutes per pound.

Refrigerate immediately. The next morning the turkey will be ready to prepare for cooking.

Although it may seem tempting to avoid the time and work of these two methods, *never defrost a turkey at room temperature.* The bird will become a breeding place for harmful bacteria.

Small turkeys can also be defrosted in the microwave oven. The bird must be unwrapped and placed in the roasting pan you eventually will cook it in. Shield thin or bony areas with small pieces of aluminum foil and rotate the bird several times during defrosting. Consult the oven manufacturer's instructions for thawing times.

Frozen, prestuffed turkeys (which we do not recommend) should *not* be thawed before cooking. Do *not* refreeze turkey unless it still contains ice crystals; otherwise cook the turkey immediately.

FRESHER IS BETTER

Frankly, we much prefer cooking a fresh turkey. As much as modern technology has perfected the flash-freezing method, we have still found a good fresh-killed bird to be superior to its frosty cousin.

Some people like to point to the lower price per pound for frozen turkey, but the difference is not that great. And if you are going to go to all the trouble required to make a Thanksgiving feast, why skimp on the most important part of the whole meal?

On occasions where circumstances required it, we have prepared frozen turkeys, and they have been good. But we always felt they would have been better if they had been fresh.

Go to your butcher or wherever you buy meat and place your order several weeks before Thanksgiving. Most meat departments don't have the room to stockpile a bunch of bulky fresh turkeys in the refrigerator, so they will order from a wholesaler or producer only as many as are spoken for. Don't get caught short.

Do not take delivery of your fresh turkey before Wednesday of Thanksgiving week. Home refrigerators—no matter how fancy they may be—do not offer the right degree of cool or humidity for lengthy storage. When you bring your turkey home, follow the instructions above that call for immediately changing the bird's wrappings.

Before cooking, remove the wrappings, rinse the turkey thoroughly under cold, running water, and pat dry with paper towels. Then you are ready to prepare the bird for cooking. If you want to bring the turkey to room temperature before cooking, drape with wax paper and let sit on a well-ventilated kitchen counter for no more than 1 hour.

ROASTING THE TURKEY

After rinsing and drying, the easiest method for preparing a turkey is to secure the flap of skin over the neck opening with a poultry pin or round wooden toothpick. Place the drumsticks in the precut band of skin, into a hock lock, or tie them together loosely.

Tuck the wing tips back under the shoulders of the bird to allow the turkey to rest more solidly on the roasting rack (this also prevents over-browning of the wing tips during roasting).

Place the turkey breast side up on an adjustable V-shaped roasting rack set in a shallow roasting pan. The rack should hold the turkey at least ½ inch above the bottom of the pan to allow the oven heat to circulate evenly around the turkey. Roasting pans with high sides inhibit heat circulation, thus increasing roasting time.

We do not recommend the kind of roasting thermometer that stays in the bird during cooking, but if you are using one, insert it into the center part of the thigh next to the body. Make sure it is not touching a bone. Brush the turkey with vegetable oil, butter, or a combination of both to prevent the skin from drying out.

Place the turkey in the center of a preheated 325-degree oven. The relatively low roasting time is the secret to a golden, juicy bird. Drippings will not burn and the meat will shrink less. Higher temperatures may cause the outside of the bird to cook faster than the inside and result in tough, dried-out meat that is difficult to carve.

Set the turkey in the middle of the oven, running lengthwise from side to side, not back to front. Halfway through the roasting process, turn the turkey around, 180 degrees, to ensure even cooking.

If the turkey achieves the proper color before the roasting time is exhausted, cover the bird with lightweight foil, shiny side down, to shield the skin against overbrowning.

HOW LONG?

There is no exact formula for the amount of time a turkey should cook, but there are general guidelines. These times are inexact because there are a number of variables that affect the roasting process. Ovens vary in size, heat distribution can be different for each oven, turkeys have individual physical characteristics, and oven temperature is directly affected by the number of times the oven door is opened. If you are cooking a bird that has been defrosted, the exact degree of thawing will also have an impact.

Here are the approximate roasting times for a turkey in a 325-degree oven:

Weight	Unstuffed	Stuffed
6 pounds	2½ hours	2¾ hours
7 pounds	2¾ hours	3¼ hours
8 pounds	3 hours	3½ hours
9 pounds	3¼ hours	3¾ hours
10 pounds	3½ hours	4 hours
11 pounds	3¾ hours	4¼ hours
12 pounds	3¾ hours	4¼ hours
13 pounds	4 hours	4½ hours
14 pounds	4 hours	4½ hours
15 pounds	4¼ hours	4¾ hours
16 pounds	4¼ hours	4¾ hours
17 pounds	4¼ hours	4¾ hours
18 pounds	4½ hours	5 hours
19 pounds	4½ hours	5 hours
20 pounds	4¾ hours	5¼ hours
21 pounds	4¾ hours	5¼ hours
22 pounds	5 hours	5½ hours
23 pounds	5¼ hours	5¾ hours
24 pounds	5¼ hours	6 hours
25 pounds	5¼ hours	6¼ hours

Remember, these are just approximations. The only way to tell if your turkey is done is to take its temperature by inserting a thermometer—the instant-reading kind—in the upper thigh area. When the internal temperature of the meat is 170 to 175 degrees, the turkey is done.

Another way to tell is to look at the juices that flow from the spot where the thermometer punctures the skin. If they run clear the turkey is done.

If you end up with a turkey that has one of those pop-up gizmos that are supposed to signal when the bird is done, ignore it. We have found that most of the time these things lead to overcooked turkeys. The indicators tend to err on the side of overdone. You can use them, but still take the turkey's temperature at the appropriate times. Frankly, we always remove those things before cooking.

TO STUFF OR NOT TO STUFF?

We have been on both sides of the big stuffing question. For a while we believed strongly that the stuffing should be cooked outside the bird. Then we switched sides and started stuffing our turkeys again.

The arguments on the side of stuffing cooked outside the turkey are (1) the turkey cooks faster and more evenly without stuffing; (2) there is much less chance of bacterial spoilage if the stuffing is kept out of the bird; and (3) the stuffing itself cooks up crisper and can be more easily controlled when it has its own separate casserole.

The arguments on the side of stuffing cooked inside the turkey are (1) this is the traditional method; (2) it is easier to do; (3) it looks great when presented; (4) the stuffing tastes better because it absorbs the flavors of the cooking turkey, and the ingredients of the stuffing flavor the turkey; and (5) the stuffing is moist and always the right temperature.

Frankly, we like it both ways. We love stuffing so much that we always make enough to fill the neck cavity, the large inner cavity, and a casserole cooked alongside the turkey. If we are particularly ambitious, we have been known to stuff the neck and the main cavity with two different kinds of stuffing.

There are important rules that must be observed when dealing with stuffing: Make sure the stuffing has been refrigerated or is, at least, cool before putting it into the turkey. Do not stuff a turkey until just before you are ready to cook it. And, be sure to remove the giblet bag from inside the turkey before stuffing.

When stuffing the turkey (or other birds) spoon the stuffing in loosely. Don't overstuff. Stuffing expands during cooking and if it is too firmly packed it is liable to split the turkey.

If you are cooking all the stuffing or some of the stuffing outside of the turkey, put it into a buttered casserole or soufflé dish, being sure to keep it loosely packed. The stuffing should not be cooked as long as you cook the turkey. An hour or less at 325 degrees should be enough to warm the stuffing through.

To keep the stuffing moist, baste the casserole occasionally when basting the turkey, and keep it covered with aluminum foil.

If you have cooked the stuffing inside the turkey, remove all of it from the bird and store the leftovers in a separate container. Leaving stuffing in the turkey carcass is an invitation to bacterial spoilage.

TRUSSING

The classic method for preparing a turkey is to truss it. This involves tying the legs and wings close to the bird's body. The reasons for trussing are

cosmetic: to make the bird look plump and round; practical: to make the turkey easier to carve and to keep it from drying out.

First tie the legs together by looping a long piece of string under the tail. Cross the string over the tail then coil it around the ends of the drumsticks. Bend the second wing joints back. Draw the string tight around the thighs and along the sides of the body and pull it through the notches in the folded wings. Turn the turkey over and tie the string across the back.

If you use a V-shaped rack some of this trussing may be unnecessary. The sides of the rack force the bird into the shape that trussing achieves. It presses the legs and wings against the body and plumps up the breast. The only trussing that may be necessary is the tail-drumstick loop described above.

CLOSING A STUFFED BIRD

One of the most daunting of Thanksgiving tasks may be the securing of the turkey once it is stuffed. Closing the cavity can be a terrifying prospect but it isn't actually that difficult.

The traditional method is to sew the opening closed using kitchen twine and a poultry needle. This is quite effective, but a bit tedious. We have found skewers to be much easier to handle. Most kitchen stores and supermarkets sell poultry skewers made especially for this purpose. They are sharply pointed 4-inch metal pins, two or three of which can easily close a turkey's main cavity.

Place the skin on one side of the cavity over the skin on the other side. Punch the skewer through both thicknesses of skin, press down on the skewer's end, and force its point back through the two pieces of skin. This will efficiently hold the opening closed. Use other skewers whenever needed to completely close off the cavity. Use the same technique on the neck opening.

When the bird is cooked, the skin has lost its elasticity. The skewers can be slipped out of their places and the cavity will remain closed.

BASTING

Keeping the turkey moist while it's cooking is an important consideration. One way to ensure this is to baste the bird. This procedure—occasionally spooning liquid over the turkey—serves several purposes. It keeps the turkey skin moist and tender. It also can help the browning process.

Any number of liquids can be used for basting, but the most common is chicken or turkey stock. As the liquid runs off into the roasting pan, it blends with the rich pan drippings from the turkey. If you use a bulb baster, you can suck up this enriched stock and baste the turkey with it.

The basting liquid in the bottom of the roasting pan helps to keep the oven environment humid (thus keeping the turkey from drying out) and it prevents drippings from burning in the pan and causing unwanted smoke and a burned taste.

Basting is helpful, but don't overdo it. Basting the bird every 20 or 30 minutes or so is plenty. Remember, each time you open the oven door the temperature inside the oven is lowered and cooking time is lengthened.

A method that Andy's mother used frequently was to soak a double thickness of cheesecloth in chicken fat or butter and drape it over the turkey breast. This holds the fat and the basting liquids against the skin of the turkey longer, and basting can be done less frequently. This method is effective, but it is important not to let the cheesecloth dry out. If it does, it will stick to the turkey skin and tear it when removed. If you use this method, remove the cheesecloth 30 minutes before the cooking time is over to brown the breast.

If you end up with a bird that describes itself as "self-basting" this doesn't mean that basting can be given up completely. The "self-basting" turkeys are injected with liquid that keeps the meat moist internally during cooking. But the skin still requires attention, and an occasional baste with stock and pan juices will keep it from drying out.

We are amazed that the government allows the free-wheeling use of the word *butter* applied to some of these self-basters when the liquid used is usually mostly vegetable oil and various chemicals, such as MSG.

TURNING

In a perfect world, the best way to cook a turkey evenly is to turn it over at one point during the process. It makes sense in theory, but just try turning a slippery 16-pounder without dropping it or tearing the skin. Turning a turkey is risky for two people and virtually impossible to do alone.

We do suggest turning the roasting pan about halfway through the cooking process. Whichever way you position the turkey (we like to place it sideways), turn it 180 degrees to roast it evenly.

RESTING

When the turkey is removed from the oven it should not be carved and eaten immediately. The bird needs to rest for 15 or 20 minutes to allow juices to redistribute themselves.

CARVING

There are several methods for carving the turkey and each has its passionate adherents.

Method 1—Traditional

This is the standard way of carving the turkey. It is particularly suited to a presentation at the dinner table in front of the gathered celebrants.

1. First remove the drumstick and thigh on one side by pulling the leg away from the body. Cut the joint near the body with a long, sharp, flexible knife.
2. Separate the drumstick from the thigh by cutting through the tendons at the knee joint.
3. Slice the dark meat off the thigh by cutting even pieces parallel to the bone, ¼-inch thick. Place the cut meat on a warm platter.
4. You can cut off the wing at this point. If you choose to do so, bend it back, away from the body, and cut at the joint.
5. Starting at the ridge at the top of the breast, slice off a slab of meat and skin about ⅛-inch thick. Continue to slice the breast, keeping the knife blade parallel to the turkey's rib cage. Be sure to keep the slices thin.
6. When you finish one side, reverse the bird and repeat the process.

Method 2—In the Kitchen

If you are carving in the kitchen, out of sight of the guests, this is an efficient method.

1.–4. Follow procedures used in Method 1 above.
5. Start at the breastbone ridge—the keel bone—above the breast. Cut down and deep, keeping the blade as close to the rib cage as possible. Following the contour of the bird, remove the entire half breast.
6. Place the half breast on a cutting surface and slice evenly against the grain of the meat. Repeat the procedure with the other half of the breast.

Method 3—The Lateral Cut

This is a clever way to cut clean, regular slices easily. It is also a good method if you are carving in front of a crowd.

1.–4. Cut off the drumstick, thigh, and wings, as in Method 1 above. Make a deep, lateral cut below the breast and parallel with the platter. This allows you to cut straight down instead of following the contour of the turkey.

5. Begin slicing about 2 inches above the cut. Slice off a ⅛-inch-thick piece and continue cutting in the same way, working your way up to the breastbone.

6. Repeat this procedure on the other side of the turkey.

BONED TURKEY

If you work carefully, you can slip off the skin of a chicken just like a glove. Unfortunately, turkeys don't work the same way because they are too big and their bones are too hard. To bone a turkey you must slit the skin down the back, remove the bones, and reattach the two sides.

The ideal size turkey for boning is 12 pounds or so. Do not attempt this on a turkey larger than 15 pounds.

Set the turkey on a flat surface, breast side down, with the neck cavity facing you. Cut the skin down the center of the backbone from the neck to the tail. Using a sharp boning knife and your fingers, peel the meat back on both sides of the cut.

When you reach the wings and legs, dislocate them and sever the tendons that hold them. Slide the knife down the wishbone and remove it. Continue scraping the meat from the rib cage on both sides until you reach the breastbone. Lift out the turkey's whole frame.

To remove the thighbone, slide your knife down the shaft of the bone, then cut the tendons at the knuckle. Leave the drumstick bones and the wings intact.

Lay the turkey skin side down on a flat surface. Place the filling in a line down the center of the turkey. Roll up the skin and sew or skewer it closed at the top.

A boned turkey is usually filled with a dense stuffing called a forcemeat (see page 73).

Turkey with Molasses Glaze

*T*his is our basic turkey recipe. We have experimented with other temperatures and other glazes, but this has been the most successful! at our table. The glaze gives the bird a deep mahogany color and its adds flavor to the skin. The slow cooking temperature keeps it moist and tender.

Serves 12, with plenty of leftovers

One 16-pound turkey, fresh or
   fully defrosted
Salt and freshly ground pepper
1 recipe Sausage-Crouton Stuffing
   (see page 61)

2 tablespoons molasses
2 tablespoons soy sauce

1. Preheat the oven to 325 degrees. Rinse the turkey inside and out with cold water. Dry thoroughly with paper towels. Sprinkle the cavity with salt and pepper. Stuff loosely (stuffing expands during cooking) and close the opening with metal skewers. Also stuff the neck cavity and skewer it closed. (Place the leftover stuffing in a buttered soufflé dish and bake it alongside the turkey for the last hour of its cooking time, basting the stuffing occasionally with pan juices.)

2. Tie the turkey's legs together and place it on a rack (we use a Teflon-coated V-shaped rack) set in a large roasting pan.

3. Mix the molasses and soy sauce in a small dish. (Variation: Use 2 tablespoons of maple syrup instead of molasses.) With a pastry brush, paint the turkey with the mixture, lifting it up to reach the under side. This method makes the bird very dark, very quickly, so the turkey should either be tented when dark or it could be first painted 2 hours before cooking is done.

4. Place the turkey in the center of the preheated oven and roast, basting occasionally with accumulated pan juices, until a thermometer inserted into the thickest part of the thigh registers 170 degrees and juices run clear. This should take between 4½ and 5 hours. The turkey skin should be quite dark. Check at the 4-hour point and if it isn't, brush again with the molasses mixture.

5. Transfer the turkey to a platter or carving board and let it rest for 20 minutes before carving.

Upside-down Turkey

$\mathcal{T}$his is a cumbersome and sometimes exasperating procedure, but the result is worth all the trouble. This may be the moistest and most delicious turkey of all. We do not advise trying this with a turkey any bigger than 12 pounds.

The idea here is to roast the turkey breast side down to make the breast meat very juicy. An hour or so before the end of the cooking time, the bird is reversed so the breast can brown properly. This is the difficult part. We have found that it really requires two people to turn the bird over without damaging the skin.

Serves 12, with leftovers

2 cloves garlic, minced	½ teaspoon freshly ground
½ teaspoon chopped fresh	pepper
rosemary	6 tablespoons unsalted butter,
½ teaspoon chopped fresh	softened
marjoram	One 12-pound fresh turkey
½ teaspoon chopped fresh	Stuffing of your choice
thyme	2 cups dry white wine
2 tablespoons chopped fresh	Chicken Stock (see page 77) for
basil	basting
½ teaspoon salt	

1. In a food processor bowl, combine the garlic, herbs, salt, and pepper with the softened butter. Purée for a few seconds to combine well. Set aside.

2. Preheat the oven to 325 degrees. Starting around the main body cavity, carefully slip your hand under the turkey skin and break the membranes that hold it to the body. With your fingers, smear the herb butter under the skin.

3. Stuff the turkey loosely, in the neck and main cavity, and close the flaps with skewers. Rub the remainder of the herb butter over the skin of the turkey. Set the turkey, breast side down, on a buttered Teflon-coated V-shaped rack set in a shallow roasting pan. Pour the wine in the pan under the turkey.

4. Roast the turkey in the preheated oven for the suggested time (see chart, page 38). Baste occasionally with stock and make sure that the liquid in the pan does not evaporate.

(continued)

5. An hour or so before the turkey is done, slide the roasting pan out of the oven and reverse the turkey. (We have found that using serving spoons is an effective way of doing this, but don't try to do this alone, if you can help it.) Another way sacrifices a clean pair of oven mitts, but seems to be foolproof and reduces the risk of dropping the bird or piercing its skin with objects. Working quickly before juices penetrate the gloves, use heat-proof, heavy gauge oven mitts to pull the pan out of the oven and directly handle the bird.

Turkey Roasted in a Paper Bag

This all-American version of the classic French *papillote* technique helps the bird retain all its moisture. If you hate dried-out turkey (who doesn't?) this is a surefire antidote.

This technique is best suited to a smaller turkey (or a chicken or capon).

NOTE: Some paper bags contain unwanted chemicals. Check at health food stores for all-natural bags.

Serves 8

One 10- or 11-pound turkey, at
   room temperature
Salt and freshly ground pepper
4 cups any stuffing (see pages
   57–73)
2 tablespoons unsalted butter,
   softened

3 carrots, coarsely chopped
3 stalks celery, coarsely chopped
2 medium onions, coarsely
   chopped
2 cloves garlic, sliced
2 bay leaves
Chicken Stock (see page 77)

1. Preheat the oven to 325 degrees. Rinse the turkey under cold, running water and then pat it dry with paper towels. Sprinkle the neck cavity and main cavity with salt and pepper. Fill each with your choice of stuffing, loosely packed. Seal each with poultry skewers. Tuck the wings under the turkey.

2. Rub the softened butter all over the turkey. Season lightly with salt and pepper. Take a sturdy, clean brown paper bag big enough to hold the turkey, and spray the inside with water. Pour out any excess water. Gently slip the turkey into the bag, facing the neck cavity forward and the legs near the opening. Roll up the opening to seal.

3. Sprinkle the carrots, celery, onions, garlic, and bay leaves evenly over the bottom of a roasting pan that is just big enough to hold the turkey. Put the giblets (except for the liver) in among the vegetables. Add chicken stock to the roasting pan to a depth of ½ inch. Place the closed bag in the roasting pan on top of the vegetables. Make sure the turkey is sitting breast side up.

4. Roast in the preheated oven for 2½ hours. Then gently roll back the bag and insert a meat thermometer into the thickest part of the leg or the thigh. The temperature should read 155 degrees. If it doesn't, roll up the bag and return the turkey to the oven for 15 minutes more. When the temperature registers 155 degrees, tear open the paper bag and raise the oven heat to 425 degrees.

5. Roast the turkey for another 30 minutes, basting occasionally. When done, the turkey should register 170 to 175 degrees on the meat thermometer and the skin should be golden brown.

6. Remove the roasting pan from the oven and transfer the turkey to a platter and cover it loosely with foil. Discard paper bag. Let the turkey sit for 20 minutes before carving.

7. Pour the pan juices through a sieve into a saucepan. Press the solids with a wooden spoon to extract their juices. Place the saucepan over medium heat, and reduce the pan juices until they thicken and form a gravy that coats the spoon. (This can be used as a base for a gravy, or it can be used on its own.)

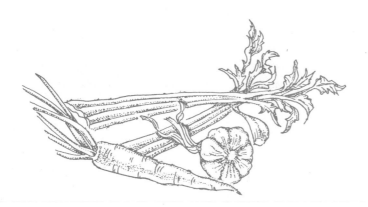

Grilled Turkey

*I*f the weather outside isn't hideous, cooking the turkey on the outdoor barbecue is a good idea. It frees the kitchen oven for other Thanksgiving goodies and it cuts down on cleanup. The grill imparts a delightful smoky nuance to the turkey and to its stuffing.

Our Los Angeles pal Laurie Burrows Grad grills her turkey poolside. Although a quick dip is not necessarily a part of Thanksgiving, temperate weather certainly brings more of the holiday party outside. Her method is simple and logical and the result is really delicious.

Laurie allows 13 to 15 minutes per pound for a stuffed turkey, about 11 minutes per pound for a turkey that is unstuffed. But she notes that outside conditions—wind direction, temperature, and humidity—can affect the timing. So can the nature of your grill. If you are using a gas or electric grill, follow the manufacturer's instructions for the use of indirect heating methods.

Be sure to choose a bird that isn't too big for your grill. You need to allow at least 1 inch between the turkey and the lid and sides of the grill. Actually, a turkey cooked on a grill should not exceed 12 pounds.

If you are using a regular charcoal kettle-style grill, you can get a rich, smoky flavor by soaking about 2 cups of mesquite chips in water for about 1 hour. Put a 12 by 9-inch disposable foil drip pan in the bottom of the grill. Build a fire of about 30 briquettes (not the self-starting kind) on the long sides of the drip pan. Light the coals and let them burn for 30 minutes with the grill uncovered. When the coals are covered with white ash, the fire is ready. Sprinkle the mesquite chips over the coals and start cooking your turkey.

On a gas grill set the heat at moderate around the outside and off in the center.

Prepare the turkey as described in general turkey instructions (pages 35–36).

Place the turkey breast side up in the center of the grill over the drip pan. Cover the grill and cook, adding 9 briquettes to each long side of the drip pan every hour.

The turkey is done when a meat thermometer inserted in the thigh registers 170 to 175 degrees. The center of the stuffing should read at least 160 degrees.

Transfer the turkey to a cutting board and let it stand 20 to 30 minutes before carving.

Roasted Split Turkey

This is good for a small group. It provides the complete traditional feast —light and dark meat and pan gravy, and very little left over. Split the turkey from the breast bone to the tail and freeze the other half. (If this seems daunting, ask the butcher to do it.)

Serves 4 to 6

½ teaspoon salt
½ teaspoon freshly ground
   pepper
One 7½-pound half turkey

1 tablespoon soy sauce
1 tablespoon maple syrup

1. Preheat the oven to 425 degrees. Salt and pepper the turkey on both sides. Place the stuffing in the breast cavity and place the turkey, cut side down, in a roasting pan.

2. Mix the soy sauce and maple syrup together. Using a pastry brush, paint the turkey skin with the mixture. Bake the turkey for 15 minutes in the preheated oven.

3. Reduce the oven temperature to 350 degrees. Roast for 1 hour, basting every 15 to 20 minutes with turkey stock or melted butter. The turkey is done when a thermometer inserted in the thickest part of the breast or thigh reaches 165 to 170 degrees. Remove from the oven and let rest for 15 minutes before serving.

4. When you lift the turkey out of the roasting pan, the stuffing will remain in the pan. Transfer it to a serving dish and then carve the turkey.

Roast Turkey Thighs with Corn Bread Stuffing

$\mathcal{T}$he Four Seasons Clift Hotel in San Francisco is open every year for Thanksgiving. Since most customers prefer white meat, chef Kelly Mills has developed this recipe for the kitchen staff. By boning out the thigh, a small roast is created that is easy to stuff and even easier to slice.

Serves 8 to 10

1 pound fresh or canned chestnuts
½ cup coarsely chopped dried cranberries
2 cups crumbled Basic Corn Bread (see page 140)
2 beaten eggs
3 tablespoons chopped fresh sage
2 tablespoons chopped fresh parsley
1 cup Chicken Stock (see page 77)

2 turkey thighs (about 3¼ pounds)
Salt and freshly ground pepper
2 tablespoons butter
4 medium shallots, minced
The turkey giblets, minced
½ cup red wine
2 cups reduced Turkey Stock (see page 78)

1. If you are using fresh chestnuts, cut a slit in each one and place in a 2-quart saucepan. Cover with water, bring to a boil over medium heat, and cook for 20 minutes. Let the chestnuts cool in the cooking water until they can be handled. The chestnuts must be moist to be peeled. Remove both outer shell and the brown skin, then chop them coarsely. You should have about 2 cups.

2. In a large bowl, combine the chopped chestnuts, cranberries, corn bread, eggs, sage, parsley, and stock. Toss gently with a fork, being careful to keep the stuffing fluffy. Set aside.

3. With a sharp boning knife, working on each thigh with its skin side down, make a cut along the length of the bone, then peel back the meat from there. Be careful to keep the knife close to the bone. Keep the meat intact and do not pierce the skin. Once the bone is removed, spread out the thigh, making slits in the meat, if necessary, to allow it to lay flat. Place the meat between 2 sheets of wax paper and pound to make them an even thickness.

4. Preheat the oven to 375 degrees. Season the thighs with salt and pepper. Place some stuffing in the middle of each butterflied thigh, in a line running lengthwise. Roll the thighs around the stuffing, and tie them with string in three or four places.

5. Place the thighs side by side (but not touching) in a shallow roasting pan. Roast for about 30 minutes, then transfer to a platter in a warm oven while you prepare the sauce.

6. Place the roasting pan over medium heat. Add the butter, shallots, and giblets to the pan, and sauté for 3 minutes. Add the wine and deglaze the pan, loosening any encrusted bits with a wooden spoon. Reduce the liquid by half and add the stock. Simmer for 20 minutes. Adjust the seasonings.

7. Untie the roasts and slice in rounds about ½ inch thick. Top with sauce and serve.

Stuffed Turkey Breast

*T*his is an ideal dish for those who have a fear of carving in front of a crowd but don't mind a bit of preparation.

Serves 6

One 5- to 6-pound turkey breast
½ teaspoon salt
½ teaspoon freshly ground
   pepper
½ teaspoon ground cinnamon
½ teaspoon ground allspice
1 tablespoon fresh thyme, or 1
   teaspoon dried

¼ teaspoon ground cloves
¼ teaspoon ground mace
½ teaspoon ground cardamom
4 cups any stuffing (see pages
   57–73)
4 strips bacon

1. The turkey breast must be boned and butterflied. You can ask your butcher to do this for you, or try it yourself. Here's how: First remove the wishbone, which is located at the front of the breast between the wings. Holding the breast in one hand with the small pointed end resting on the cutting board, scrape the meat at the top of the breast with the blade of a boning knife. Once the knife touches bone, use your fingers to loosen the V-shaped end and pull out the bone.

Lay the breast skin side down on the cutting board. Insert the tip of a very sharp boning knife between the meat and the rib cage, about 1 inch down on each side to loosen the muscle. Using your hands, gently pull the breast meat away from the rib cage, toward the center bone.

Turn the breast over and continue loosening the meat from the bone. The meat is firmly attached to the bone by cartilage; to avoid tearing, use the knife to cut the connective tissue as you work your fingers between the meat and bone. This should yield a large, flat piece of meat.

Often the muscle next to the separation in the breast bone will not come off in one piece with the top of the breast. To remove this muscle, slip the tip of the boning knife under the fillet on each side of the bone and pull the section free. If you have to remove this fillet separately, it can be stuffed in the roll or frozen for later use.

To even out the meat, place it skin side down on the cutting board, cover with wax paper, and pound to flatten it.

2. Combine all the seasonings and rub over the surface of the turkey. Refrigerate for at least 2 hours, preferably overnight.

3. When ready to cook, preheat the oven to 400 degrees. Lay the turkey skin side down on a flat surface. Place the stuffing of your choice along the center. Bring both sides of the breast together around the stuffing, forming a long shape about 2 to 3 inches in diameter and 12 to 14 inches long. Tuck one side under the other to form a very tight roll, and either sew, skewer, or tie it with string like a roast. Cut a piece of aluminum foil long enough to cover the roast with a few inches to spare.

4. Butter the foil. Place the strips of bacon the length of the roast on top and wrap tightly. Twist the ends of the foil to secure the wrap. Place the roast seam side up in a baking pan. Bake in the preheated oven for 40 minutes.

5. Reduce the oven temperature to 350 degrees. Peel back the foil and bake for 20 minutes, or until golden brown. If you wish, you can baste the roast once or twice with a combination of stock and butter or oil.

6. Remove from the oven. Let rest 5 to 10 minutes, remove strings or skewers, and cut in slices ¼ inch thick. Serve with the juices that collect in the foil or with a gravy of your choice.

Stuffed Cornish Game Hens with Zinfandel Gravy

*T*here is something appealing about each guest getting his or her own whole bird to feast on. Cornish game hens are another purely American addition to the realm of poultry. In this case, the plump little birds are a result of crossing Plymouth Rock hens with various types of small game birds. They are always available frozen, and frequently you can find them fresh.

Serves 6

6 Rock Cornish game hens
1 lemon, cut into sections
Salt and freshly ground pepper
6 cups Chicken Liver Stuffing
    (see page 69)
6 strips bacon

½ cup (1 stick) unsalted butter,
    melted
2 cups good Zinfandel
1 cup Chicken Stock (see page 77)
2 tablespoons flour
2 tablespoons water

1. Preheat the oven to 350 degrees. Rinse the birds under cold running water, and dry with paper towels. Rub the cut sections of lemon inside and outside the birds. Sprinkle with salt and pepper inside and out.

2. Loosely stuff each bird with 1 cup of stuffing. Sew or skewer closed.

3. Cut each strip of bacon in half and lay two halves on each bird's breast in an X.

4. Place the birds on a rack in a low-sided roasting pan. Place in the preheated oven and roast for 1 hour. Use a bulb baster to baste frequently with the melted butter and any pan juices.

5. Transfer hens to a warm serving platter. Pour off the fat in the roasting pan.

6. In a saucepan over moderate heat, combine the wine and stock and bring to a boil. Reduce to a simmer.

7. Put flour and water in a container with an airtight lid. Shake vigorously to mix. Strain mixture and then pour into stock and wine mixture. Stir constantly until it begins to thicken.

8. Place roasting pan over heat and pour in the thickened stock. Stir constantly with a wooden spoon, scraping the entire pan to loosen the baked-on juices. Season the sauce to taste. Pour into a gravy boat or spoon over the hens. Serve immediately.

Roast Duck Stuffed with Couscous

$\mathcal{W}$hat to serve for a small Thanksgiving party is always a question. The smallest turkey you can buy will serve 6 or even 8 people. This means you will need something smaller—unless you want to be working on leftovers for a week or so.

If you are just two or perhaps four, you'll need to find something other than turkey. A roast chicken will certainly do the trick, but if you are interested in something a bit more festive, we recommend duck.

Duck is mighty rich, but for this special day it is quite appropriate. The fattiness can be reduced while roasting and cut with the use of a tangy kumquat cranberry compote.

Serves 2 as a full meal, or 4 as part of a big holiday feast

One 5-pound duck	1 tablespoon soy sauce
1 lemon, cut in half	1 tablespoon maple syrup
Salt and freshly ground pepper	
3 cups Couscous Stuffing (see page 68)	

1. Remove the neck and giblets from inside the duck. Reserve them to make stock. Rub the duck inside and out with the lemon halves. Pierce the skin all over with the tines of a fork to speed the loss of fat during cooking. Liberally sprinkle the bird with salt and freshly ground pepper inside and out.

2. Preheat the oven to 400 degrees. Stuff the duck cavity with Couscous Stuffing and close the opening with skewers. Place some stuffing in the neck cavity and close. Tie the legs together with string and place the bird on a rack in a sturdy baking pan.

3. Combine the soy sauce and maple syrup in a small dish and paint the mixture all over the duck with a pastry brush. Roast for 15 minutes, then reduce the heat to 350 degrees. Bake for 1 hour, or until the juices run clear when you pierce the thigh with a skewer. If the duck gets too brown, cover with foil. Serve.

Roast Goose

Serves 6

One 11- to 13-pound goose,
  fresh or frozen
1 tablespoon salt
1 tablespoon freshly ground
  pepper
1 lemon, cut in half

Port, Apricot, and Rice Stuffing
  (page 72)
2 cups Goose (see page 78) or
  Chicken Stock (see page 77)
Port and Currant Jelly Sauce
  (see page 85)

1. If using a frozen goose, thoroughly defrost it by storing in the refrigerator for 38 hours. Remove from the refrigerator, place on a platter, and bring the bird to room temperature (this should take about 4 hours).

2. Three hours before serving, prick the skin all over with a sharp fork and rub the exterior and interior of the goose with the lemon halves. Cut off the wing tips at the second joint. Preheat the oven to 350 degrees.

3. Sprinkle the goose inside and out with salt and pepper. Stuff the bird loosely and leave the cavity open. Put a small amount of stuffing in the neck cavity and skewer it closed. If you have extra stuffing, put it in a baking dish and cook it alongside the bird, basting occasionally. Either tie the legs together or make a slit in the skin above the tail that is large enough to insert the ends of the legs.

4. Set the goose, breast side up, on a rack in a roasting pan. Baste every 20 minutes with stock. Remove fat periodically from the pan with a bulb baster or spoon. Cook for 2½ hours, or until a meat thermometer inserted in the center of the upper thigh registers 180 degrees.

NOTE: It may be necessary to cover the goose with foil to prevent over-browning, but if you use such a cover, take it off for the last 10 minutes of cooking time to give the bird a glossy golden brown finish.

Stuffing

We guess that if a vote were taken in our house for the most popular part of the Thanksgiving feast, stuffing would win hands down. The rich mix of flavors and textures make a good stuffing delicious and make it one leftover that never lasts more than a day.

Stuffing is a self-contained side dish. Its close contact with the turkey (or other poultry) creates a strong bond. The turkey takes on the flavors of the stuffing, and the stuffing absorbs the juices and flavors of the turkey. In fact, stuffing is the ideal vehicle for adding seasonings to the essentially monochromatic turkey.

The American stuffing or, as those nineteenth-century puritans who found the word risqué would have it, "dressing" is loosely packed in the cavities of the poultry. It is served as a vegetable. Most stuffings are usually based on a starch—bread, bread crumbs, rice, potatoes—and they are seasoned with herbs, nuts, fruits, and other interesting items.

The probable ancestor of American stuffing is forcemeat (from the French, *farcir,* "to stuff"), a dense mixture of ground meat, spices, and herbs. The difference between the two is the fact that forcemeat is tightly packed and is usually cut and served as part of the bird. Stuffing is scooped out and served on the side.

The key thing to remember about stuffing is to keep it cool and never stuff a turkey or other poultry in advance. Stuff only when you are ready to put the bird in the oven. If not handled correctly, stuffing can become a ripe medium for bacteria.

STUFFING THE TURKEY

The general rule is to allow ¾ to 1 cup of moistened stuffing per pound of dressed-weight turkey. Another way to arrive at the amount is to multiply the number of servings by ¾ cup.

Stuffing should be kept airy and not compressed when filling the cavities of the turkey or other poultry. The action of heat and moisture during cooking causes stuffing to expand and, in an extreme case, might cause an overstuffed turkey to burst. Keep in mind that extra stuffing can be tucked into the neck cavity.

This table indicates how much stuffing is normally required for birds of certain weights. It is difficult to be exact with these amounts because the size of turkey cavities varies considerably. Nevertheless, this should be a helpful guideline.

Bird Size	Approximate Amount of Stuffing
2 to 4 pounds	2 cups
4 to 6 pounds	4 cups
6 to 8 pounds	5 cups
8 to 10 pounds	6 cups
10 to 12 pounds	8 cups
12 to 15 pounds	10 cups
15 to 20 pounds	12 cups
20 to 25 pounds	16 cups

This should not intimidate stuffing lovers who want to make much more than will fill a bird. They can place the excess stuffing in a covered casserole and bake it alongside the turkey for about 1 hour. Cooked stuffing may be frozen and kept for 3 or 4 weeks.

Quick Stuffing

Makes 6 cups

2 tablespoons unsalted butter
1 clove garlic, minced
¼ cup chopped red onion
¼ cup diced celery
1 tablespoon fresh sage, or 1
    teaspoon dried
¼ teaspoon fresh rosemary, or
    pinch of dried

1 cup fresh or frozen peas
1 cup stock
5 cups of crisp, dry bread cubes
    made from white or corn
    bread
1 egg, lightly beaten (optional)
½ cup chestnut halves

1. In a skillet, melt 1 tablespoon butter. Sauté the garlic and onion for 1 minute. Add the celery, seasonings, and peas. Sauté for 2 minutes to warm. Add the stock and bring the mixture to a simmer over medium heat. Cook for 5 minutes.

2. Remove the vegetables from the skillet with a slotted spoon. Reserve. Raise the heat, bring the liquid still in the skillet to a boil, and reduce to ¾ cup.

3. In a large mixing bowl combine the bread and the vegetables. Spoon the reduced liquid over the stuffing and toss gently. The stuffing should hold together. If it doesn't, add an egg and toss with a fork to combine.

4. In a skillet, melt the remaining butter, add the chestnuts and sear. Add to the stuffing mixture and toss again to combine. Refrigerate until ready to use.

ADVANCE PREPARATION: Can be prepared 2 days ahead. Cover and refrigerate. Bring to room temperature before using.

Sausage-Crouton Stuffing

$\mathcal{W}$e developed this stuffing for *Bon Appétit* magazine. Frankly, we thought of the name first, then created the recipe to go with it. This is a rich, earthy, and extremely delicious stuffing with great texture.

Makes 16 cups

1¼ pounds challah or other egg bread, crusts trimmed, cut into ½-inch cubes
1 pound sweet Italian sausage, casings removed
1 medium onion, chopped
4 celery stalks, chopped
½ cup drained canned water chestnuts, quartered
½ cup (about 2 ounces) toasted and coarsely chopped pecans

2 tablespoons chopped fresh parsley
4 teaspoons chopped fresh sage, or 1½ teaspoons ground dried
¼ cup Chicken (see page 77) or Turkey Stock (see page 78)
2 tablespoons unsalted butter, melted
Salt and freshly ground pepper

1. Preheat the oven to 300 degrees. Spread the bread cubes in a single layer on 2 large cookie sheets. Bake until crisp, about 20 minutes. Transfer to a large bowl.

2. Crumble the sausage meat into a large skillet, and sauté over medium heat until cooked through, about 12 minutes. Add to the bread crumbs, using a slotted spoon.

3. In the same skillet, sauté the onion and celery until transparent, about 10 minutes. Add to the bread mixture. Mix in the water chestnuts, pecans, parsley, and sage. Add the stock and butter and toss to combine (the mixture will be dry). Season with salt and freshly ground pepper.

ADVANCE PREPARATION: Can be prepared 1 day ahead. Cover and refrigerate. Bring to room temperature before using.

Glazed Chestnut, Apple, and Sausage Stuffing

Makes about 8 cups

4 ounces veal sausage
4 ounces pork sausage
½ onion, chopped
2 celery stalks, chopped
8 slices stale honey wheat berry
  or whole wheat bread
1 cup Goose (see page 78) or
  Chicken Stock (see page 77)
5 tablespoons dry white wine
2 teaspoons sugar

1 cup canned chestnuts broken
  into large pieces
1 cup chopped tart green apple,
  either Granny Smith or
  Pippin
1 egg, beaten
2 teaspoons dried ground sage
¼ cup chopped fresh parsley
Salt and freshly ground pepper

1. Crumble sausages in chunks into a medium skillet set over medium heat, and sauté until just brown. Add onion and celery and cook until the celery is bright green, about 5 minutes.

2. Preheat the oven to 250 degrees. Place the bread slices on a cookie sheet and bake until crisp, about 15 minutes. Remove from the oven and cut into 1-inch squares. Combine with sausage mixture and toss gently.

3. In a small sauté pan combine the stock and white wine and reduce by half over moderate heat. Stir in the sugar and simmer for a few minutes longer. Toss the chestnuts in the glaze until completely coated. Remove with a slotted spoon, then repeat the procedure with the apples.

4. Add the chestnuts and apples to the sausage mixture along with the egg, sage, and parsley. Season to taste with salt and pepper, and mix gently with a fork, being careful to keep the stuffing fluffy, not compressed. (If the stuffing is too dry, add a dash of wine or stock to moisten it. If you are using fresh sage, double the amount.)

ADVANCE PREPARATION: Can be prepared 1 day in advance. Cover and refrigerate. Bring to room temperature before using.

Corn Bread Stuffing

$\mathcal{T}$here are people in our family who dote on stuffing. We suspect they might even like stuffing better than the turkey itself. One year Andy helped himself and was halfway through dinner, paying special attention to the large pile of stuffing on his plate, when he realized that he had completely forgotten to serve himself some turkey. "I never missed it," he said licking his lips. This was the stuffing in question.

Makes 8 cups

¼ cup chicken or turkey fat or
    butter
3 medium onions, chopped
3 stalks celery, sliced
2 cloves garlic, minced
2 eggs, well-beaten
1 cup Chicken (see page 77) or
    Turkey Stock (see page 78)
½ cup minced fresh parsley

4 cups of crumbled Basic Corn
    Bread (see page 140), dried
    out either in a turned-off oven
    overnight or in the dry air
½ cup chopped walnuts
½ cup chopped water chestnuts
    (optional)
Salt and freshly ground pepper

1. Melt the fat or butter in a medium skillet. Sauté the onions, celery, and garlic until the vegetables are translucent but not brown. Add the eggs, stock, and parsley. Stir to combine.

2. Place the corn bread in a large bowl and add the onion and celery mixture. Add the walnuts and water chestnuts, if desired. Season to taste with salt and pepper. Toss to combine, being careful not to compress the stuffing any more than necessary. Keep it fluffy. Cover the bowl and refrigerate until ready to use.

ADVANCE PREPARATION: Can be prepared 2 days ahead. Cover and refrigerate. Bring to room temperature before using.

Oyster Corn Bread Stuffing

*A*lthough it sounds trendy, oyster stuffing has been traditional Thanksgiving fare for a very long time. We found it in some cookbooks published in the late nineteenth century. This version adds a few twists, including corn bread and Paul Prudhomme's idea of prebaking the stuffing before putting it into the bird. This gives it a deep mahogany color.

Makes 6 cups

Two 10-ounce containers of
   oysters and their liquor
2 cups cold water
2 teaspoons minced garlic
¾ teaspoon salt
¾ teaspoon cayenne
¾ teaspoon paprika
¾ teaspoon freshly ground
   pepper
½ teaspoon dried oregano
½ teaspoon dried thyme
2 cups diced onions

1¼ cup finely diced celery
¾ cup chopped red bell pepper
⅔ cup thinly sliced leeks, white
   only
8 tablespoons (1 stick) unsalted
   butter
⅔ cup chopped fresh parsley
2 small bay leaves
2 cups crumbled Basic Corn
   Bread (see page 140)
½ cup chopped scallions

1. In a bowl, combine oysters, their liquor, and cold water. Stir and chill at least 1 hour. Remove the oysters from the liquid and reserve separately; refrigerate until ready to use.

2. In a small bowl, combine 1 teaspoon minced garlic with the seasonings and reserve.

3. In another bowl, combine the onions, celery, bell pepper, and leeks. Toss to mix thoroughly. In a medium sauté pan, over high heat, melt half the butter and add half the vegetables (2⅓ cups), reduce heat to medium, and sauté 30 minutes to brown the onions thoroughly. Stir occasionally.

4. Reduce the temperature to low. Add half of the garlic seasoning mixture and the remaining minced garlic, and sauté 4 minutes, stirring constantly and scraping the bottom of the pan.

5. Add the remaining butter and turn the heat to high. Add the rest of the vegetables, ⅓ cup parsley, and the bay leaves. Sauté for 10 minutes, stirring occasionally.

6. Preheat the oven to 350 degrees. Stir the reserved oyster liquid into the vegetable mixture, and simmer for 15 minutes. Add the remaining

seasonings and stir. The corn bread should be added ½ cup at a time to make a fairly moist stuffing. Remove from the heat. Fold in the oysters, being careful not to break them. Spoon stuffing into an ungreased 8 by 8-inch baking pan. Bake in the oven for 1 hour. After 30 minutes, when a dark crust appears, stir. Scrape from the sides and bottom of the pan. When finished baking, remove bay leaves.

7. Add the rest of the parsley and the scallions, stirring well. Cool the stuffing and refrigerate, being sure to chill it well before it is to be used.

ADVANCE PREPARATION: Can be prepared 1 day ahead. Cover and refrigerate. Bring to room temperature before using.

Sauerkraut Apple Stuffing

$\mathcal{K}$it Snedaker is a great editor and food historian. She found this slightly oddball but quite delicious 1949 stuffing recipe. This stuffing is best with duck or goose.

Makes 12 cups

6 cups coarse, fresh bread
  crumbs
3 cups sauerkraut, drained
2 cups diced apples, (Granny
  Smith or other tart variety
  does best)

1 cup chopped onions
½ teaspoon caraway seed
1 tablespoon grated orange zest

1. Spread the bread crumbs in a jelly-roll pan and bake in a 250-degree oven for 10 minutes.

2. Combine the bread crumbs with the remaining ingredients, and mix well.

ADVANCE PREPARATION: Can be prepared 2 days ahead. Cover and refrigerate. Bring to room temperature before using.

Pistachio and Apple Stuffing

*T*he price of these nuts makes this stuffing almost as decadent as bathing in Dom Perignon. But we present this recipe unashamedly because it is exceptionally delicious.

Makes 12 cups

½ cup currants
¼ cup Calvados or apple jack
¼ cup extra-virgin olive oil
6 cups cubed French bread, crust on
2 cups shelled pistachio nuts
8 tablespoons (1 stick) unsalted butter
3 celery stalks, trimmed and diced
3 medium onions, coarsely chopped
1½ cups sliced mushrooms
3 cloves garlic, minced

½ teaspoon freshly grated nutmeg
½ teaspoon paprika
½ teaspoon dried thyme, or 1 teaspoon fresh
¼ teaspoon cayenne
Salt
2 tart apples, such as Granny Smith, peeled, cored and cut into small chunks
Juice of 1 lemon
½ cup Chicken (see page 77) or Turkey Stock (see page 78) (optional)

1. Place the currants in a small bowl and pour the Calvados or apple jack over them. Let soak 1 hour.

2. In one or two skillets, heat 1 or 2 tablespoons olive oil and brown the bread cubes, turning them several times. Add more olive oil, as needed.

3. Preheat the oven to 350 degrees. Toast the nuts for 8 minutes in a single layer on a baking sheet or a jelly-roll pan lined with foil. Cool and reserve.

4. Melt 4 tablespoons butter in a large skillet over medium heat. Sauté the celery and onions until transparent, about 5 minutes. Add the mushrooms, garlic, and seasonings. Sauté, stirring occasionally, for 3 more minutes. Transfer to a large bowl.

5. In another bowl, moisten the apple chunks with the lemon juice. Add to the onion mixture, and toss to combine. Add the bread cubes and nuts, and toss again to combine.

6. Melt the remaining butter in the skillet and dribble it over the stuffing. If you wish, moisten the mixture with chicken stock, but be careful not to let the stuffing become soggy. Correct seasoning.

ADVANCE PREPARATION: Can be prepared 1 day ahead. Cover and refrigerate. Bring to room temperature before using.

Knickerbocker Corn Bread Stuffing

Peggy Knickerbocker is a successful San Francisco restaurateur and caterer. Her stuffing recipe is a real stunner.

Makes 16 cups

1 pound sliced bacon
2 cups celery, cut into small dice
2 medium yellow onions, finely chopped
1 head garlic, cloves peeled and finely chopped
3 red bell peppers, seeded and cut into small dice
1½ teaspoons dried sage
1½ teaspoons dried marjoram
1½ teaspoons dried thyme
1½ teaspoons dried oregano
Basic Corn Bread (see page 140), dried out either in a turned-off oven overnight or in the dry air
¼ cup Marsala
1 teaspoon salt
Freshly ground pepper

1. Cook the bacon until crisp. Remove from the pan and reserve. Pour off the drippings, leaving ½ cup in the pan. Over medium heat, sauté the vegetables in the fat, but don't let them get too soft. They should retain a little crunch. Add the dried herbs. (If you can get fresh herbs, double the quantities.)
2. In a large bowl crumble the corn bread and bacon. Add the vegetable mixture with its cooking fat, the Marsala, salt, and pepper to taste. Stir to moisten and combine the ingredients.

ADVANCE PREPARATION: Can be prepared 1 day ahead. Cover and refrigerate. Bring to room temperature before using.

**Thanksgiving
Dinner**

Couscous Stuffing

*T*he combination of couscous, corn, and garlic makes an unforgettable stuffing for small birds. We love it with duck, but it does equally well with chicken, game hens, and small turkeys.

Makes about 5 cups

1½ cups Chicken Stock (see page 77)
2 tablespoons unsalted butter
¼ teaspoon salt
1 cup whole wheat couscous
2 tablespoons olive oil
2 large shallots, finely chopped
2 small celery stalks without leaves, finely chopped (about ¼ cup)
3 baby carrots, finely chopped (about ¼ cup)

1 clove garlic, minced
¼ cup corn kernels, fresh or frozen
¼ cup pine nuts, toasted
½ cup minced fresh parsley
1 tablespoon fresh sage
1 teaspoon Bell's Seasoning, or ½ teaspoon dried oregano and ½ teaspoon dried thyme
Salt and freshly ground pepper

1. In a 1-quart saucepan combine the stock, butter, and salt. Bring to a boil over medium heat. Add the couscous in a steady stream and stir. Reduce to a simmer and cook for 5 minutes. Fluff the couscous with a fork and set pan aside in a warm place.

2. In a medium skillet, heat the oil. Lightly sauté the shallots, celery, and carrots for 2 minutes. Add the garlic and sauté for another minute. Spoon into a medium mixing bowl.

3. Add the couscous, corn, pine nuts, parsley, sage, and Bell's Seasoning to the vegetables. Toss to combine (don't press too hard, try to keep the stuffing fluffy). Add salt and pepper to taste.

ADVANCE PREPARATION: Can be prepared 2 days ahead. Cover and refrigerate. Bring to room temperature before using.

Chicken Liver Stuffing

$\mathcal{T}$his rich stuffing is best with small birds, chicken, squab, and game hens. It is loaded with flavor and interesting textures.

Makes about 12 cups

1 pound chicken livers	2 cups long-grain rice
4 tablespoons unsalted butter	4 cups Chicken Stock (see
1 medium onion, minced	page 77)
1 teaspoon salt	8 ounces baked ham, cut in
½ teaspoon freshly ground	small dice
pepper	½ cup shelled pistachio nuts
1 tablespoon chopped fresh sage,	(optional)
or 1 teaspoon dried	¼ cup minced fresh parsley

1. In a medium saucepan, sauté the chicken livers in the butter until just barely done, about 5 minutes. Remove the livers from the pan with a slotted spoon. Chop them coarsely and reserve.

2. Add the minced onion to the saucepan. Stir to coat with the butter, cover, and cook over low heat for 8 minutes, stirring occasionally, until translucent. Add salt, pepper, and sage. Add the rice and stir over moderate heat for a few minutes, until the rice becomes translucent.

3. In a separate saucepan, bring the chicken stock to a boil. Pour the stock into the rice mixture, reduce heat to low, and cover. Let simmer for about 20 minutes, until all the liquid has been absorbed and the rice is tender but not mushy.

4. Stir in the chicken livers, ham, nuts, and parsley. Correct the seasonings.

ADVANCE PREPARATION: Can be made 1 day ahead. Cover and refrigerate. Bring to room temperature before using.

Sausage, Prune, and Rice Stuffing

*T*his is a delicious combination that provides harmonious texture and admirable flavor. We like to use this for stuffing smaller turkeys or other birds such as game hen or capon.

Makes about 12 cups

1 pound good quality pork
    sausage
½ cup currants
1 cup best quality soft prunes
2 cups minced onions
3 tablespoons unsalted butter
    (optional)
1 teaspoon salt
½ teaspoon freshly ground
    pepper

1 tablespoon fresh thyme, or 1½
    teaspoons dried
2 cups long-grain rice
4 cups Chicken Stock (see
    page 77)
3 tablespoons chopped fresh
    parsley

1. Prick the sausages all over and place them, with ½ cup of water, in a large saucepan. Cover and simmer over low heat for 5 minutes. Uncover, drain off the water, and sauté the sausages for several minutes, until lightly browned. Remove the sausages, saving the drippings in the pan, and chop them coarsely. Place in a large mixing bowl. (If the sausage casings are too tough, strip them off and crumble the meat into the bowl.)

2. Put the currants and prunes into separate bowls and cover each with very hot water. Let soften for 15 minutes.

3. Over medium heat sauté the minced onion in the sausage drippings in the saucepan. Stir the onion to coat with fat; if there is not enough fat, add the butter. Cover and cook over low heat for 8 minutes, stirring occasionally, until translucent. Add salt, pepper, and thyme. Add the rice and stir over moderate heat for a few minutes, until the rice becomes translucent.

4. In a separate saucepan, bring the chicken stock to a boil. Pour the stock into the rice mixture, reduce heat to low, and cover. Let simmer for about 20 minutes, until all the liquid has been absorbed and the rice is tender but not mushy.

5. Drain the fruits. Squeeze the currants dry in a towel and add to the bowl containing the sausage. Dry the prunes on paper towels, then chop coarsely and add to the sausage mixture. Add the rice and turn the ingredients with a spoon to blend well. Add parsley. Taste for seasoning and correct if necessary. Cover and refrigerate until ready to use.

ADVANCE PREPARATION: Can be prepared 1 day ahead. Cover and refrigerate. Bring to room temperature before using.

Savory Wild Rice Stuffing

*T*his stuffing is wonderful in goose, wild or domesticated turkey, or chicken. It is also a first-class leftover, so make plenty.

Makes 16 cups

8 ounces (2 sticks) unsalted butter
2 cups wild rice
2 cups long-grain rice
3 large onions, chopped
2 cups chopped celery, including leaves
4 cups Chicken Stock (see page 77)
2 cups toasted and coarsely chopped pecans

¼ cup chopped fresh parsley
1 tablespoon salt
1 tablespoon dried sage
1 tablespoon dried marjoram
1 tablespoon dried savory
1 tablespoon ground cinnamon
2 teaspoons celery seed
1 teaspoon freshly ground white pepper

1. Melt the butter in a large heavy skillet or casserole. Add rices, onions, and celery. Cook over medium heat for 6 minutes, stirring occasionally. Add the stock and bring to a boil. Reduce the heat, cover the pot, and simmer for 25 minutes, or until the stock is completely absorbed and the rice is tender.
2. Stir in the pecans and seasonings, and mix thoroughly.

ADVANCE PREPARATION: Can be prepared 2 days ahead. Cover and refrigerate. Bring to room temperature before using.

Port, Apricot, and Rice Stuffing

*T*his is an ideal stuffing for such smaller birds as guinea hens, capons, or chickens. It works well with goose also.

Makes 8 cups

1 cup dried apricots, coarsely
    chopped
½ cup dried currants
2 cups ruby port
4 cups Chicken Stock (see page
    77)
2 tablespoons unsalted butter
2 tablespoons vegetable oil
1 cup minced onions

2 celery stalks, chopped
2 cups long-grain rice
2 tablespoons minced fresh
    thyme, or 2 teaspoons
    crumbled dried
½ cup chopped fresh parsley
1 teaspoon salt
½ teaspoon freshly ground
    pepper

1. Put the apricots and currants into separate bowls and cover each with 1 cup of port. Let soak overnight, or for at least 6 hours, at room temperature.

2. Bring the stock to a boil in a medium saucepan.

3. In a large saucepan melt the butter with the oil over medium heat. Add the onions and celery. Sauté, stirring occasionally, for 5 minutes over medium heat. Add the rice and stir until translucent, about 3 minutes.

4. Add the hot stock to the rice and mix well. Reduce the heat to low and cover. Let simmer for about 20 minutes, until all the liquid has been absorbed and the rice is tender but not mushy. Transfer to a large bowl.

5. Drain the fruits, reserving the port for Port and Currant Jelly Sauce (page 85). Combine the apricots, currants, thyme, parsley, salt, and pepper with the cooked rice. Turn the ingredients with a spoon to blend well. Taste for seasoning and adjust if necessary.

ADVANCE PREPARATION: Can be prepared 2 days ahead. Cover and refrigerate. Bring to room temperature before using.

VARIATION: Substitute a good packaged wild rice and brown rice combination for the long-grain rice.

Herb, Mushroom, and Chestnut Forcemeat

his is a forcemeat, not a standard poultry stuffing. It should be used with a boned bird—a small turkey (see page 43), a chicken or a capon—and then sliced along with it.

This recipe was suggested by Hubert Keller, a partner and the chef at Fleur de Lys restaurant in San Francisco, one of the country's finest French dining rooms. Mr. Keller is Alsatian and he was trained at the famous Auberge de L'il.

Makes 12 cups

1½ pounds boneless loin of veal
1½ pounds pork fat
10 ounces chicken livers
4 tablespoons olive oil
4 tablespoons chopped shallots
3 cloves of garlic, finely chopped
½ cup finely chopped celery
3 tablespoons port
5 tablespoons cognac
3 eggs
1 tablespoon chopped, fresh
    rosemary
1½ tablespoons chopped, fresh
    thyme leaves

2 tablespoons finely cut chives
2 tablespoons finely chopped
    parsley
Salt and freshly ground pepper
4 tablespoons pistachio nuts
½ pound cooked wild
    mushrooms (black
    chanterelles, shiitake, morels,
    cepes)
1 pound fresh, roasted, peeled
    chestnuts

1. Finely mince the veal, pork fat, and chicken livers in a meat grinder or in a food processor.

2. Heat the olive oil in a sauté pan. Add the shallots and garlic, sauté until light golden in color, then add the celery. Add the meat and cook for 5 minutes, stirring constantly. Add the port and cognac and transfer the mixture to a bowl. Let cool.

3. Stir in the eggs, herbs, salt and pepper. Check the seasoning. Delicately mix in the pistachios, mushrooms, and the chestnuts without breaking them. Refrigerate for at least 20 minutes before using. Use in a boned turkey (see recipe page 52).

ADVANCE PREPARATION: This can be prepared 1 day ahead. Cover and refrigerate. Bring to room temperature before using.

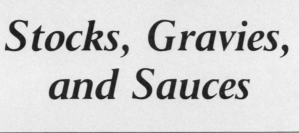

Stocks, Gravies, and Sauces

At young ages and in separate places, we both became gravy lovers. The first time you see someone make an indentation in a snowy mound of mashed potatoes with a gravy ladle, you know.

To both of us, a piece of meat on a plate without gravy or sauce is naked, incomplete. As a result, our Thanksgiving is a gravy festival. We usually have at least two, sometimes three, gravies.

Essentially, a gravy adds texture and flavor depth to the Thanksgiving plate. But a good gravy should broaden and fill out the meal, not overpower it.

The following gravies, stocks, and sauces are the elements that bind the holiday dinner together. Without them, Thanksgiving dinner would be just another meal.

Several of the recipes that follow use butter. The same amount of fat from the roasting pan is more desirable, but then the gravy must be made at the very last minute. The addition of essences from the pan may be worth the extra effort.

Chicken Stock

Chicken stock is an essential ingredient of the Thanksgiving feast (and many other special meals). We start by boiling the chicken alone so that most of the skimming can be done at the beginning of the procedure. After straining the stock, we like to boil it down even more. This makes for a richer, more concentrated stock with a reduced volume that is easier to store and to freeze. You can use it as is, or dilute with water.

Makes 3 quarts

6 pounds chicken (carcasses, feet, necks, backs, hearts, and other parts) cut into small pieces, or use a large stewing hen
5 quarts water
2 stalks celery
3 medium carrots, washed and sliced

2 leeks, most of the green part cut off, washed and split lengthwise
2 garlic cloves, crushed
2 medium onions, quartered
2 teaspoons salt
12 black peppercorns, cracked
1 bay leaf
A sprig of thyme

1. Put the chicken and the water into a large stockpot. Bring to a boil over high heat. Reduce the heat to medium and continue to boil for 20 minutes, skimming the liquid frequently with a spoon.

2. Add the rest of the ingredients. When the liquid returns to a boil reduce the heat and simmer the stock, for about 3 hours, skimming periodically.

3. Strain the stock through a fine sieve or a colander lined with cheesecloth. Return to the stockpot and boil vigorously for another ½ hour.

4. Let cool, cover and refrigerate. When the stock has chilled, use a large spoon to remove and discard the fat from its surface.

ADVANCE PREPARATION: The stock can be made 3 days in advance. Cover and refrigerate. If not using within 3 days, freeze the stock in plastic tubs (it is better to use several smaller containers so that you don't have to defrost the entire batch to use only a few cups).

Turkey Stock

Makes 6 cups

2 pounds turkey parts and giblets	12 crushed peppercorns
1 onion, quartered	4 sprigs fresh thyme, or 1 teaspoon dried
2 carrots, cut in 3-inch pieces	1 bay leaf
2 celery stalks with leaves, cut in half	8 cups cold water
	Salt

1. Place the first seven ingredients in a large stockpot, and add the cold water. Bring to a boil, reduce heat, and simmer. Skim the surface of the stock occasionally during the first 30 minutes.

2. Partially cover and continue to simmer for 3 to 5 hours.

3. Strain and salt to taste.

ADVANCE PREPARATION: Can be made 3 days ahead. Cover and refrigerate. Can be frozen for several months.

Goose Stock

Makes 6 cups

9 cups Chicken Stock (see page 77)	1 celery stalk from the heart, chopped
1 goose neck	1 bouquet garni: 6 peppercorns;
1 goose gizzard	1 celery stalk, cut in half; 2
1 goose heart	sprigs fresh thyme; and 1 bay
1 carrot, peeled and chopped	leaf

1. Make a bouquet garni by pressing the peppercorns into one half stalk of celery. Place the thyme and bay leaf on top and tie the other half stalk on top with string to make a tight sandwich.

2. Place all ingredients in a 2-quart saucepan. Bring to a boil, then simmer, uncovered, until the liquid is reduced to 6 cups, about 50 minutes. Strain.

ADVANCE PREPARATION: Can be prepared 2 days ahead. Cover and refrigerate. Can also be frozen for several months.

Basic Pan Gravy

Makes 1½ cups

3 tablespoons fat from the roasting pan	2 cups Turkey (see page 78) or Chicken Stock (see page 77)
3 tablespoons flour	Salt and freshly ground pepper

Blend the fat and flour in the roasting pan, making a smooth roux. Add the stock and bring to a boil over medium heat. Scrape the bottom of the pan with a wooden spoon to loosen baked-on bits. Stir until the sauce thickens. Add salt and pepper to taste, and serve.

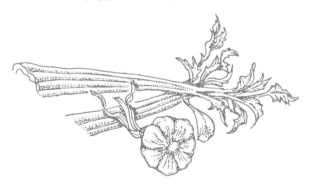

Pan Gravy

Makes 1½ cups

2 cups Turkey (see page 78) or Chicken Stock (see page 77)

1 cup red wine
Salt and freshly ground pepper

1. After removing the bird to a warmed platter to rest, pour off the fat from the turkey roasting pan. Place over medium heat and add the stock and wine to the pan.

2. Bring to a boil and use a wooden spoon to scrape up baked-on bits. Continue boiling until the liquid has been reduced by half. Add salt and pepper to taste, and serve.

Goose Pan Gravy

Makes 3 cups

4 cups Goose Stock (see page 78)
1 cup dry white wine
2 tablespoons all-purpose flour

4 tablespoons water
Goose roasting-pan drippings
Salt and freshly ground pepper

1. In a saucepan over moderate heat combine the stock and wine and bring to a boil. Reduce to a simmer.

2. Put flour and water in a container with an airtight lid. Shake vigorously to mix. Strain mixture and then pour into stock. Stir stock constantly until it begins to thicken.

3. Place roasting pan over heat and pour in the thickened stock. Stir constantly with a wooden spoon, scraping the entire pan to loosen the baked-on spots. Season to taste with salt and pepper.

Mushroom Gravy

*T*his and most other gravies are greatly enhanced by the addition of defatted and deglazed pan drippings from the turkey.

Makes 4 cups

4 ounces mixed dried wild
   mushrooms or dried porcini
   mushrooms
6 cups Turkey (see page 78)
   or Chicken Stock (see page 77)
4 tablespoons unsalted butter
2 carrots, peeled and diced
1 medium onion, diced

1 celery stalk, chopped
1 pound sliced white
   mushrooms
⅔ cup Madeira
1½ teaspoons chopped fresh
   thyme, or ½ teaspoon dried
Salt and freshly ground pepper

1. In a bowl, cover the dried mushrooms with warm water and let stand 30 minutes. Remove mushroom pieces with a skimmer, then strain liquid through several thicknesses of cheesecloth, a paper towel, or a coffee filter, reserving the liquid.

2. In a 2-quart saucepan, reduce the stock to 3 cups to make a rich base for the gravy.

3. In a medium skillet, melt 3 tablespoons butter and add carrots, onion, and celery. Sauté over low heat until the vegetables are soft, about 15 minutes. Stir occasionally to prevent sticking.

4. Add half the sliced white mushrooms to the skillet. Sauté until tender, about 10 minutes. Add Madeira, reduced stock, and mushroom-soaking liquid. Bring to a boil over medium-high heat, reduce heat, and simmer for 10 minutes.

5. Pour the mixture into a blender and purée until smooth.

6. In the 2-quart saucepan, melt the remaining butter. Add the wild mushrooms and the remainder of the white mushrooms. Sauté until golden brown.

7. Add the purée, thyme, and salt and pepper to taste.

ADVANCE PREPARATION: Can be prepared several days in advance. It will keep, covered and refrigerated, for 3 days. If you are using pan drippings, they must be added at the last minute.

Our Favorite Gravy with (or Without) Giblets

*T*his gravy must be started the day before Thanksgiving, but it's really easy, and we promise you've never tasted anything better. Our children, who have a tendency to be suspicious of sauces, can't get enough of this one.

The recipe allows us the option to finish the sauce with or without the minced giblets. The kids like the gravy without "lumps" and the adults generally like the morsels. We are able to offer two gravies from this one recipe by adding the giblets to only half of the finished product.

Makes about 4 cups

Turkey giblets (neck, gizzard, liver, heart)
1 celery stalk
2 medium carrots, washed and cut into 2 pieces
A few fresh sprigs parsley

3 cups Chicken (see page 77) or Turkey Stock (see page 78)
½ cup chicken fat, turkey fat, or butter
½ cup all-purpose flour
Salt and freshly ground pepper

1. The day before you plan to serve the gravy, simmer the giblets, celery, carrots, and parsley in the stock for about 1½ hours, or until the gizzard is tender.

2. Strain the stock into a bowl. Discard the vegetables. Remove the gristle from the gizzard and discard it. Strip the meat from the neck. Chop the neck meat, the gizzard, and the liver into slivers about ½ inch long. Place the chopped giblets in a bowl with enough broth to cover. Store it overnight, covered, in the refrigerator. Refrigerate the rest of the stock in a separate bowl, covered.

3. The next day, heat the reserved stock in a saucepan.

4. In a medium saucepan, melt the fat or butter over medium heat, add the flour, and stir well to make a smooth, thick roux. Let bubble for a few minutes.

5. Remove the saucepan from the heat, add the heated reserved stock, and simmer for 20 minutes until the sauce coats a spoon and no taste of flour remains. Add salt and pepper to taste.

6. At this point, you can separate the desired amount of gravy and add the reserved giblets to it.

7. When you remove the turkey from the oven, strain the pan drippings into a pitcher or a gravy separator. Defat and add to the gravy. Correct the seasonings. Deglaze the pan with the remaining ½ cup of stock.

VARIATION: For a richer and even more chunky gravy, sauté 8 ounces of chicken livers in 1 tablespoon of fat or butter until they are browned. When they are cool, chop them finely and reserve them in a bowl. Deglaze the pan with ½ cup stock, and reserve the liquid. Add the livers and their liquid to the gravy with the giblets.

Roasted Garlic–Herb Gravy

Makes 1 quart

2 carrots, peeled	4 tablespoons chopped fresh
2 celery stalks	Italian parsley
2 heads garlic, cloves separated	1 tablespoon chopped fresh
and peeled	chives
8 cups Turkey (see page 78) or	1 teaspoon chopped fresh savory,
Chicken Stock (see page 77)	or pinch of dried savory
1 teaspoon salt	
½ teaspoon freshly ground	
pepper	

1. In the last hour of turkey roasting, scatter the carrots, celery, and garlic in the bottom of the roasting pan.

2. In a 3-quart saucepan, bring the stock to a boil over medium heat. Reduce by half.

3. When the turkey comes out of the oven, remove the carrots and celery stalks and place them in a blender or food processor. Add the stock and purée until smooth. Add half the garlic cloves, purée, and taste. (Heads of garlic vary in intensity, so it is necessary to check the strength of the sauce as you go.) Add more garlic to taste, if desired.

4. Stir in the salt and pepper, and just before serving, add the parsley, chives, and savory.

Chestnut Gravy

Makes 1 quart

2 tablespoons unsalted butter
2 carrots, peeled and diced
1 celery stalk, chopped
1 medium white onion, chopped
1½ cups whole peeled and
  cooked chestnuts

2 tablespoons brandy
⅔ cup red wine
6 cups Turkey (see page 78) or
  Chicken Stock (see page 77)

1. In a 3-quart saucepan, melt the butter and sauté the carrots, celery, and onion until tender, about 15 minutes. Add 1¼ cups of chestnuts and continue to cook, stirring frequently, for 1 minute.

2. Add the brandy and wine and deglaze the pan while rolling chestnuts around in the liquid. Add the stock, bring to a simmer, and reduce for 30 minutes.

3. Purée the gravy in a blender or food processor until smooth. Quarter the reserved chestnuts. Stir the remaining chestnuts into the gravy. Serve.

ADVANCE PREPARATION: Can be made 3 days in advance. Refrigerate, covered, until ready to use. Warm in saucepan.

Orange-Port Sauce

Makes 4 cups

8 tablespoons (1 stick) unsalted
  butter
2 carrots, peeled and chopped
1 celery stalk, chopped
2 medium white onions,
  chopped
4 cups Turkey (see page 78) or
  Chicken Stock (see page 77)

1⅓ cups tawny port
1 cup fresh orange juice
1 tablespoon red wine vinegar
2 tablespoons chopped fresh
  thyme, or 2 teaspoons dried
Salt and freshly ground pepper

1. In a 3-quart saucepan, melt 2 tablespoons butter. Sauté carrots, celery, and onions until tender, about 15 minutes.

2. Add the stock, port, and vinegar and reduce by half, about 20 minutes.

3. Meanwhile, in a small saucepan, reduce the orange juice by half, to intensify its flavor. Reserve.

4. Transfer the port mixture to a blender or food processor and purée. Strain back into the saucepan. Over medium heat, add the remaining butter in small pieces, stirring constantly. Do not boil.

5. Add the orange juice, thyme, and salt and pepper, plus any available pan juices from the turkey roasting pan.

ADVANCE PREPARATION: Can be made 3 days in advance. Store, covered, in the refrigerator. Warm in a saucepan.

Port and Currant Jelly Sauce

This sauce is the companion to Roast Goose (page 56) and Port, Apricot, and Rice Stuffing (page 72). If you are using the stuffing, use the port in which you soaked the apricots in this recipe.

Makes 3 cups

2 cups apple cider or sparkling   1 cup port
   apple cider   1 cup currant jelly
4 cups Goose (see page 78) or
   Chicken Stock (see page 77)

In a 2-quart saucepan, boil the cider, reducing it to 1 cup. Add the goose stock and port. Bring to a rolling boil and then lower to a fast simmer for 20 minutes. Add jelly ½ cup at a time. Stir to blend. The sauce should be thick enough to coat the back of a spoon.

ADVANCE PREPARATION: Can be made 3 days in advance. Cover and refrigerate until ready to use. Warm in a saucepan.

Vegetables

*I*f the turkey is the backbone of Thanksgiving dinner, then vegetables are the heart. At our house the feast includes one or two turkeys and anywhere from six to nine vegetable dishes. There are so many wonderful vegetables available at this time of year that choices can be difficult. We generally try to avoid these difficult decisions by making as many vegetables as we can fit on the plate.

Perhaps the best way to choose is to zero in on specific categories. For example, pick one sweet potato dish, one potato dish, one squash, one green vegetable, and one other that you just can't resist. Another important consideration is to make sure that you have several recipes that can be prepared in advance.

Also, think about color. There's nothing worse than four or five dishes all of which are brown or orange. Try to choose things that will complement one another in color and texture.

Thanksgiving is a celebration of the bounty of the harvest and vegetables are the expression of that bounty.

Broccoli au Gratin

This is always a popular dish at our house. It has a lovely color and a good texture. The kids love the crispy cheese crust.

Makes 6 cups (12 ½-cup servings)

3 pounds broccoli, peeled, cut
    into fairly large and relatively
    uniform pieces
3 tablespoons unsalted butter
3 medium shallots, minced
2 cloves garlic, minced
⅔ cup sour cream

1 cup grated Parmesan cheese
½ teaspoon freshly grated
    nutmeg
½ teaspoon freshly ground white
    pepper
½ teaspoon salt

1. In a 4-quart saucepan, bring 4 cups of salted water to a boil. Add the broccoli and boil for 5 minutes. Strain into a colander and spray with cold water to stop the cooking process. Chop coarsely.

2. Melt the butter in a skillet. Sauté the shallots for 3 minutes, stirring frequently. Add the garlic and sauté for another minute.

3. Add the shallot mixture to the bowl of a food processor fitted with the metal blade. Pulse a few times to purée. Add the sour cream and pulse 4 or 5 times to mix. Add the broccoli and ¾ cup of the Parmesan, and pulse 4 or 5 times. The mixture should not be overpuréed. Stir in the nutmeg, pepper, and salt.

4. Preheat the broiler. Spoon the broccoli mixture into a 2-quart au gratin or soufflé dish. Sprinkle the top with the remaining grated Parmesan. Place under the broiler for 2 minutes, or until the cheese is melted and slightly golden. Serve.

ADVANCE PREPARATION: Can be done 1 day in advance through step 2.

Creamed Onions

*T*his traditional dish is controversial. For some, it wouldn't be Thanksgiving without creamed onions; others couldn't care less. One of the problems with the dish is that most recipes for it yield a very bland and uninspiring result. This version is so delectable, thanks to the bechamel sauce, that even confirmed creamed onion haters have been known to have seconds.

Makes 8 cups (16 ½-cup servings)

2 pounds small white onions,
    uniform in size
5 tablespoons unsalted butter
1½ teaspoons fresh thyme, or ½
    teaspoon dried

1 cup Turkey (see page 78) or
    Chicken Stock (see page 77)

BECHAMEL

2 tablespoons unsalted butter
3 tablespoons all-purpose flour
2 cups milk
1 cup heavy cream
½ teaspoon freshly ground white
    pepper
½ teaspoon salt
2 teaspoons freshly squeezed
    lemon juice

½ teaspoon Dijon mustard
¼ teaspoon freshly grated
    nutmeg
⅓ cup freshly ground bread
    crumbs, preferably sourdough
    or egg bread
⅓ cup grated Parmesan cheese

    1. Parboil the onions, timing 1 minute after the water comes to a boil. Peel the onions and cut an X in the root end of each to prevent bursting.

    2. Melt 2 tablespoons butter in a 12-inch skillet, add the onions and the thyme, and sauté for 5 minutes. Add 1 cup turkey or chicken stock and bring to a boil over medium heat. Reduce the heat, cover, and simmer until the onions are tender, about 20 minutes. Check occasionally to make sure the liquid doesn't boil away.

    3. While the onions are braising, make the bechamel. In a 2-quart saucepan set over medium-low heat, melt 2 tablespoons butter and whisk in the flour. Cook for 2 minutes, but don't let the roux brown.

    4. In another saucepan, scald the milk and cream. Add a few drops to the flour roux and whisk until smooth. Continue adding the milk-cream mixture in small amounts, whisking after each addition, until all of it is

incorporated and smooth. Continue to stir until the sauce thickens, about 5 minutes. Remove the sauce from the heat and whisk in the pepper, salt, lemon juice, mustard, and nutmeg.

5. Preheat the broiler. Pour one-third of the sauce into a shallow 3-quart casserole or gratin dish. Spoon the onions into the dish and top with the remaining sauce. Mix the crumbs and cheese in a small dish, and sprinkle them over the onions. Dot with 3 tablespoons butter and place under the broiler until the crumbs begin to brown and the cheese melts, about 2 minutes, and serve.

ADVANCE PREPARATION: The bechamel and the onions can each be prepared 2 days in advance. Cover and refrigerate separately. Bring to room temperature before heating in a 300-degree oven, assemble, and begin with step 5.

Green Beans in Hazelnut Butter

$\mathcal{A}$ quick, last-minute recipe.

Serves 12

2 pounds of green beans, preferably small *haricots verts*	½ cup hazelnuts, toasted and skinned
8 tablespoons (1 stick) unsalted butter	Salt and freshly ground pepper

1. Bring 2 quarts of water to a boil in a saucepan. Trim the ends off the beans and add them to the boiling water. Cook over moderate heat for 2 to 5 minutes, or until the beans are just tender. Pour into a colander, and immerse in a large bowl of cold water.

2. Melt the butter in a skillet large enough to accommodate all the beans. Add the beans and sauté for 2 minutes, stirring and tossing frequently. Add the chopped hazelnuts. Stir to combine, and sauté for another minute. Add salt and pepper to taste. Transfer to a warmed serving dish and serve immediately.

ADVANCE PREPARATION: Can be prepared through step 1 one day ahead. Cover and store at room temperature.

Thanksgiving Dinner

The Best Spinach Ever

$\mathcal{W}$e're not kidding about this. We guarantee you have never tasted anything quite as purely delicious. Yes, there happens to be a considerable amount of fat in this spectacular dish, but once or twice a year shouldn't hurt. (Actually, eating this masterpiece is worth any small risk.) The flavor and texture is palate boggling.

This dish, which is attributed to the great French gourmet Brillat-Savarin, takes four days to make, but the actual work time is minimal. In order to prepare for Thanksgiving, you need to start the recipe on the Monday before.

Makes 4 cups (12 ⅓-cup servings)

5 pounds fresh spinach	Freshly ground pepper
1 pound (4 sticks) unsalted butter	Freshly ground nutmeg (optional)
Salt	

1. Rinse the spinach under cold running water. Do not dry. Place a large soup kettle or stockpot over medium heat. Grab a handful of spinach and, after shaking off excess water, put it into the pot. When the first batch has steamed and wilted, push it aside and add another handful. Continue this procedure, pushing all the cooked spinach around the sides and leaving a well in the middle for the cooking of subsequent handfuls.

2. When all the spinach has been cooked, let the spinach cool until you are able to handle it without burning your hands. Then pick it up in handfuls and firmly squeeze out the water. Chop the spinach coarsely.

3. Melt 1 stick of butter in a large skillet. Add the squeezed and chopped spinach, and sauté until all the butter is absorbed. Season with ½ teaspoon salt.

4. Place the spinach in a glass bowl, cover, and refrigerate overnight.

5. The next day, repeat the procedure using another stick of butter. Sauté the spinach until the butter is completely absorbed. Return to the glass bowl, cover, and refrigerate overnight.

6. Repeat the procedure the following day, using the third stick of butter.

7. On the day the spinach is to be served, remove it from the refrigerator 2 hours before dinnertime. Repeat the absorption procedure for the

final stick of butter and add the pepper and optional nutmeg. Taste carefully before adding any more salt. Cover and keep at room temperature until ready to serve.

8. When ready to serve, place the spinach in the skillet one more time, and sauté the spinach briefly to warm through.

Creamed Spinach

$\mathcal{T}$his is so simple we almost didn't include it, but our daughter Amanda brought us to our senses. Go a little easy on the salt because cream intensifies its flavor.

Makes 6 cups (12 ½-cup servings)

8 tablespoons (1 stick) unsalted butter	2 cups heavy cream
Four 10-ounce packages frozen spinach, thawed and chopped	Salt and freshly ground pepper
	Freshly grated nutmeg

1. In a large skillet melt the butter over moderate heat, then add the spinach. Toss until all the spinach is coated and no liquid remains.

2. Add 1⅓ cups of the cream. Stir and allow the spinach to absorb the cream before adding more. Repeat until all cream is used. Season to taste with salt and pepper. Just prior to serving, sprinkle with nutmeg.

Garlic, Spinach, and Rice Casserole

*N*atalie Grunewald was a well-known San Francisco decorator in the 1950s. Her rice casserole recipe is still a mainstay in the Thanksgiving menu of her daughter, Ingrid Kornspan. We like to serve this as a vegetable, but it also works well as a stuffing.

Makes 10 cups (20 ½-cup servings)

¼ cup olive oil
2 heads garlic, peeled and finely minced
3 medium onions, finely chopped
2 cups long-grain rice
3 cups Chicken Stock (see page 77)

Two 10-ounce packages chopped spinach, thawed
1 cup grated Parmesan cheese
½ teaspoon freshly ground pepper

1. Warm the olive oil in a large heavy skillet over medium heat. Sauté the garlic and onions until soft. Add the rice and sauté until all the ingredients are lightly browned. Add the stock, bring to a boil, reduce heat, cover, and simmer for 20 minutes, or until the rice has softened and absorbed all the liquid.

2. Preheat the oven to 350 degrees. Take the spinach in handfuls and squeeze out as much water as you can. Put the spinach in a food processor fitted with the metal blade and pulse 4 times to chop finely. Stir the spinach into the rice with ½ cup cheese and the pepper. Sprinkle the remaining cheese over the top of the casserole.

3. Bake for 15 minutes.

VARIATION: If you want to use this as a stuffing, make in the same way, just eliminate the cheese.

ADVANCE PREPARATION: Can be prepared 1 day ahead through step 2. Cover and store at room temperature. Heat at 350 degrees for 30 minutes.

Peas à la Francais

$\mathcal{T}$his is a Thanksgiving vegetable that was a tradition at Kathy's family table for as long as she can remember.

Makes 6 cups (12 ½-cup servings)

4 tablespoons unsalted butter
16 pearl onions, peeled
6 large leaves Boston lettuce,
   shredded
4 cups thawed frozen green peas
¼ teaspoon dried thyme, or
   ½ teaspoon fresh
Pinch of salt and freshly ground
   pepper

2 teaspoons sugar
4 tablespoons chopped fresh
   parsley plus 2 sprigs
½ cup water
2 tablespoons all-purpose flour
Freshly grated nutmeg

1. In a medium saucepan, melt 2 tablespoons of butter and add the onions, lettuce, peas, thyme, salt and pepper, sugar, 2 tablespoons chopped parsley and the 2 sprigs, and water. Cover and simmer for 20 minutes, stirring occasionally. Remove the parsley stems when the onions are tender.

2. In a small mixing bowl, cream the remaining 2 tablespoons of butter with the flour and a grating of nutmeg, and mix thoroughly with the peas. Reduce heat to low and gently simmer for 15 minutes, stirring occasionally. Serve in a heated casserole sprinkled with the remaining chopped parsley.

ADVANCE PREPARATION: Can be prepared through the first step 1 day in advance. Cover and refrigerate. When ready to serve, do step 2.

Baby Beets with Ginger Glaze

*T*ry to find baby beets about 1½ inches in diameter. If you have to use full-sized beets, quarter them after baking.

Makes 9 cups (18 ½-cup servings)

4 pounds baby beets	1 cup Chicken Stock (see page
1 cup water	77)
4 tablespoons unsalted butter	2 tablespoons sugar
2 teaspoons freshly grated	2 tablespoons chopped fresh
gingerroot	parsley

1. Preheat the oven to 350 degrees. Place the unpeeled beets in a medium-size pot with the water and cover. Bake in the preheated oven for 40 minutes.

2. Drain the liquid into a small bowl and reserve. Peel the beets as soon as you can handle them.

3. Melt the butter in a saucepan. Sauté the ginger in the butter for 2 minutes. Add the reserved beet liquid, the chicken stock, and the sugar. Bring to a simmer and reduce until the liquid becomes syrupy. Roll the beets in the glaze. Sprinkle with parsley and serve.

VARIATION: If you can find them, use one bunch of golden beets. The contrast between the flavor and color of the two types is very appealing, but be sure to cook the different-colored beets separately as the color of the purple ones will stain the golden variety.

ADVANCE PREPARATION: Can be prepared 1 day ahead. Cover and refrigerate. Bring to room temperature before reheating.

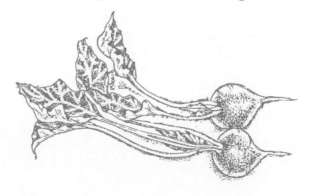

Beet and Pear Purée

$\mathcal{K}$athy loves beets. Over the years we have tried numerous beet recipes and this one is far and away the best of the lot. It has the natural sweetness of the pears, the rich and earthy flavor of beets, and a dazzling magenta color. What more could you ask?

Makes 9 cups (18 ½-cup servings)

8 medium beets
1 pound (4 sticks) unsalted
   butter
1½ cups finely minced Vidalia
   onions (about 4)
4 Bosc pears, peeled, cored, and
   minced

2 tablespoons sugar
½ cup Cranberry Vinegar (see
   page 132) or champagne
   vinegar
1 teaspoon salt

1. Preheat the oven to 375 degrees. Trim the beet tops and scrub the beets clean under running water. Put the beets in a small covered casserole with 1 cup of water. Cover and bake in the oven for 45 minutes, or until tender enough to be pierced with a fork.

2. Rinse the beets with cold water and peel them. Chop coarsely.

3. In a medium skillet melt the butter. Add the onions, pears, sugar, and vinegar. Sauté about 20 minutes or until everything is tender.

4. In a food processor fitted with the metal blade, add the onion mixture and pulse until smooth. Add salt and half of the chopped beets. Pulse again 4 or 5 times. Add the remaining beets and pulse 2 or 3 times. (This leaves some small chunks in the purée for texture.) Correct seasonings and serve.

ADVANCE PREPARATION: Can be prepared 1 day in advance and then reheated in the top of a double boiler.

Golden Winter Purée

*T*his can be served on its own or as a contrast in flavor and color to the Winter White Purée (page 102).

Makes 5 cups (10 ½-cup servings)

1 pound carrots, peeled and cut
    into 1-inch cubes
1 pound yellow turnips, peeled
    and cut into 1-inch cubes
1 firm pear, peeled, cored, and
    cut into 1-inch cubes

6 tablespoons unsalted butter
¾ cup heavy cream
½ teaspoon ground ginger
Salt and freshly ground pepper
1 teaspoon freshly grated
    nutmeg

1. Bring 4 quarts of salted water to a boil in a stockpot. Add the vegetables and pear, and boil until they are tender enough to be pierced easily with a fork, about 20 minutes. Drain in a colander.
2. Purée the vegetables and pear in a food processor fitted with the metal blade or mash with a potato ricer. Add the butter in small pieces. Add the cream and ginger. Pulse to mix thoroughly. Season to taste with salt and pepper. Spoon into a serving dish, smooth the top, and sprinkle with nutmeg.

ADVANCE PREPARATION: Can be prepared 1 day ahead. Cover and refrigerate. Bring to room temperature before baking at 350 degrees for 20 minutes.

Braised Carrots

*S*imple and delicious, this is a perfect Thanksgiving vegetable. It can be made a day ahead and warmed up in a double boiler. Be careful not to overcook; the carrots should show a bit of resistance.

Mkes 6 cups (12 ½-cup servings)

8 large carrots
4 tablespoons unsalted butter
1 cup Chicken Stock (see page
  77)

2 teaspoons sugar
Salt and freshly ground pepper
2 tablespoons chopped fresh
    chervil or parsley

1. Peel the carrots and cut them into 3-inch-long sections. Split the sections in half lengthwise and cut into sticks. Try to make the pieces uniform by varying the number cut from each piece depending on its size.

2. Melt the butter in a 12-inch skillet. Add the carrots and sauté for about 4 minutes, or until tender.

3. Add half the chicken stock and the sugar and continue to sauté over medium heat, stirring frequently. Add the rest of the stock, and season with salt and pepper to taste. Continue to sautée, stirring frequently, until the liquid has reduced to a glaze. Sprinkle with chopped chervil, correct the seasoning, and serve.

ADVANCE PREPARATION: Can be prepared 1 day ahead. Cover and refrigerate. Bring to room temperature before reheating.

Vegetables

99

Onion and Carrot Ragout

E asy and incredibly delicious, this combination provides an interesting texture contrast to most other Thanksgiving vegetables.

Makes 9 cups (18 ½-cup servings)

12 medium carrots	12 tablespoons (1½ sticks)
6 medium onions	unsalted butter
	Salt and freshly ground pepper

1. Cut the carrots into slivers 3 inches long and about ¼ inch wide. Slice the onions thinly. You should have about 6 cups of each.

2. In a medium skillet melt 6 tablespoons butter. Add the onions and sauté, stirring frequently, over medium-low heat until caramelized. This should take about 25 minutes.

3. In another skillet melt the remaining 6 tablespoons butter. Add the carrots and sauté, stirring frequently, over low heat until tender. This should take about 10 minutes.

4. Combine the carrots and onions. Toss to mix. Season with salt and pepper to taste and serve.

ADVANCE PREPARATION: Can be prepared 1 day ahead. Cover and refrigerate. Bring to room temperature before reheating.

Carrot Pudding

*O*ur friend Sue Wollack makes this delicious pudding every Thanksgiving and all throughout the year. Her kids love this dish and so do ours.

Makes 10 cups (20 ½-cup servings)

3 egg yolks	2 pounds carrots, cooked until
½ cup sugar	tender, cut into chunks
12 tablespoons (1½ sticks)	½ cup grated cheddar cheese
unsalted butter	1½ teaspoons baking powder
¾ cup flour	4 egg whites

TOPPING

2 cups walnut pieces	¼ cup sugar
2 tablespoons unsalted butter	

1. Preheat the oven to 300 degrees. In the bowl of a food processor fitted with the metal blade, or an electic mixer fitted with the paddle beater, beat the egg yolks and sugar together until light and fluffy. Alternate additions of small amounts of butter and small amounts of flour, until all are incorporated. Add carrots and cheese. Pulse to blend. Pour into a bowl and fold in baking powder.

2. Beat the egg whites until fluffy. Stir a small amount into the batter with a whisk. Fold in the remaining egg whites.

3. Pour the mixture into a buttered 3-quart soufflé dish or a 9- by 14-inch pan. Bake in the preheated oven for 30 minutes, or until a toothpick inserted in the center of the pudding comes out clean.

4. While the pudding is baking, sauté the walnuts in the butter for about 1 minute, sprinkle with the sugar, and top the pudding. Scoop out helpings and serve.

VARIATION: Top the soufflé with sour cream.

Autumn Vegetable Medley

Makes 5 cups (10 ½ cup servings)

3 large carrots, peeled	1½ teaspoons champagne
2 medium turnips, peeled	vinegar
2 medium rutabagas, peeled	½ teaspoon salt
4 tablespoons unsalted butter	½ teaspoon freshly ground
2 tablespoons flour	pepper
2 teaspoons Dijon mustard	2 tablespoons chopped fresh
1 teaspoon whole grain mustard	chervil, or 1 tablespoon dried

1. Halve the carrots lengthwise and slice them into ¼-inch half moon shapes. Place in a bowl and set aside. Cut the turnips into ¼-inch dice. Cut the rutabagas into a thick julienne. Set these two together aside in another bowl.

2. In a 3-quart saucepan, bring 3 cups of lightly salted water to a boil. Add the carrots and cover. Boil for 3 minutes, until just tender. Add the remaining vegetables, cover, and boil an additional 3 minutes. Strain through a sieve held over a bowl. Reserve the cooking liquid.

3. Return the cooking liquid to the saucepan and bring to a boil. Reduce to 1¼ cups.

4. In another saucepan melt the butter over medium heat. Stir in the flour and cook, stirring constantly, until light brown, about 1 minute. Gradually add the cooking liquid, continuing to stir. Reduce heat. Stir in the mustards, vinegar, salt, and pepper. Cook about 30 seconds more.

5. Add the vegetables and chervil to the mustard sauce. Stir to thoroughly coat the vegetables, cover, and cook over medium heat for 4 minutes. Serve immediately.

ADVANCE PREPARATION: Can be made through third step 2 days in advance. Cover and refrigerate.

Winter White Purée

This is a rich and luscious purée that transcends its humble ingredients. The apple gives the vegetables the touch of acidity and sweetness that they need. The dish works well on its own or in color and flavor contrast with the Golden Winter Purée (page 98).

Makes 6 cups (12 ½-cup servings)

1 pound white turnips	¾ cup heavy cream
1 pound parsnips	Salt and freshly ground white
1 tart green apple	pepper
½ pound cauliflower	½ cup freshly grated Parmesan
10 tablespoons unsalted butter	cheese

1. Peel the turnips and parsnips, peel and core the apple, and cut them all into 1-inch cubes. Separate the cauliflower florets.

2. Bring 4 quarts of salted water to a boil in a stockpot. Add the vegetables and apple, and boil until they are tender enough to pierce easily with a fork, about 15 minutes. Strain in a colander.

3. Purée the vegetables in a food processor fitted with the metal blade or mash with a potato ricer. Add the butter in small pieces. Add the cream. Pulse to mix thoroughly. Season to taste with salt and pepper.

4. Place the mixture in a buttered 2-quart ovenproof casserole. Smooth the top and sprinkle with the grated Parmesan.

5. Preheat the oven to 350 degrees. Bake for 20 minutes, until lightly browned on top.

ADVANCE PREPARATION: Can be prepared 1 day ahead through step 4. Cover and refrigerate. Bring to room temperature before baking at 350 degrees for 20 minutes.

Creamed Succotash

$\mathcal{A}$ colorful version of a Thanksgiving classic, this should not be made ahead of time.

Makes 5 cups (10 ½-cup servings)

2 cups fresh or frozen lima
    beans
2 cups fresh or frozen corn
    kernels
2½ cups heavy cream
3 tablespoons unsalted butter

½ cup finely diced red bell
    pepper
½ teaspoon salt
½ teaspoon freshly ground
    pepper

1. If using fresh vegetables, bring 6 cups of water and 1 tablespoon salt to a boil. Cook the corn and lima beans until tender but firm, about 5 minutes. Drain, rinse in cold water, and drain again. If using frozen vegetables, thaw thoroughly, rinse, and set aside.

2. In a large saucepan, heat the cream to a boil and reduce to 1¼ cups. This should take about 15 minutes. To prevent the cream from boiling over, place a metal spoon in the pan.

3. In a skillet, melt the butter. Add the bell pepper and sauté for 1 minute, then add the corn and lima beans. Sauté to heat thoroughly. When the cream has reduced, add the vegetables, toss to coat, season with salt and pepper, and serve immediately.

Mill Valley Corn Custard

$\mathcal{L}$iz Levy is a fine Marin County cook and this is one of her greatest creations. It is silky and extremely elegant.

Makes 6 cups (12 ½-cup servings)

1 tablespoon unsalted butter
⅔ cup finely chopped red onion
½ teaspoon cornstarch
1 cup heavy cream
4 cups fresh or frozen corn
  kernels
2 large eggs

4 egg yolks
½ teaspoon salt
¼ teaspoon freshly ground white
  pepper
1½ tablespoons chopped fresh
  chives

1. Melt the butter in a skillet and sauté the onion until softened. Cool.

2. In a bowl, combine cornstarch and cream. Stir until the cornstarch is dissolved.

3. Preheat the oven to 350 degrees. Place the onion, the corn, the whole eggs, the egg yolks, and the cream mixture in the bowl of a food processor fitted with the metal blade. Pulse until well blended. Strain the custard through a sieve, pressing down on the solids. Stir in salt, white pepper, and chives.

4. Pour the mixture into a 9½-inch au gratin dish set in a roasting pan filled with ½ inch of hot water. Cook for 25 minutes or until a knife inserted into the center comes out clean. Serve immediately.

Bix's Corn Custard

*O*ne of San Francisco's best restaurants is Bix, a stylish supperclub featuring the creative cooking of Cindy Pawlcyn. Among the appetizers on the menu is this silky corn custard. It has become a favorite. At Bix it is served set on a bed of rich shiitake mushroom sauce. For Thanksgiving the custard without the sauce is more appropriate and, as it turns out, it is excellent on its own. We include the sauce so you can try it both ways.

Serves 6

THE CUSTARD

1 tablespoon unsalted butter, softened	¾ cup grated Monterey Jack cheese
2 eggs	¼ teaspoon salt
1 cup heavy cream	⅛ teaspoon freshly ground pepper
½ tablespoon Dijon mustard	1 large scallion, finely sliced
1½ cups corn kernels (2 ears)	

THE SAUCE

6 tablespoons unsalted butter	1 tablespoon white wine
½ teaspoon finely minced garlic	½ cup of reduced Chicken Stock (see page 77)
1 teaspoon chopped shallots	3 tablespoons minced fennel leaves
¼ cup chopped fresh fennel	Salt and freshly ground pepper
¼ cup sliced shiitake mushrooms	
¼ cup champagne vinegar	

1. Preheat the oven to 325 degrees. In a bowl, combine the eggs, cream, and mustard. When smooth, fold in the remaining ingredients, except the butter. Pour into 6 buttered ½-cup ramekins. Place in a shallow baking dish filled with 1 inch of hot water. Cover with a sheet of heavy-duty foil. Bake for 30 minutes and serve immediately.

2. Melt 2 tablespoons of butter in a skillet. Sauté the garlic and shallots until soft. Do not brown. Add the fennel and mushrooms, and sauté for 2 minutes. Deglaze the pan with vinegar and wine.

3. Add the chicken stock, reduce by half, and add the rest of the butter. When the sauce is thickened, add the fennel leaves and season to taste with salt and pepper.

Schatze's Corn Pudding

*A*ndy's mother, Schatze, has been making this delicious pudding for decades. It is always the children's favorite Thanksgiving vegetable. In fact, this dish is part of nearly every family celebration in the Blue house. The recipe calls for canned creamed corn. Generally, we like to make things from scratch and not use prepared foods, but we have tested this recipe with freshly made creamed corn, and there is no appreciable difference in the final product.

Makes 8 cups (16 ½-cup servings)

8 tablespoons (1 stick) unsalted butter
4 eggs, beaten
Two 17-ounce cans creamed corn
Two 5-ounce cans evaporated milk

1 tablespoon sugar
Pinch of cayenne
6 tablespoons matzo meal
1 tablespoon salt, or to taste

1. Preheat the oven to 350 degrees. Butter a 2-quart casserole.
2. Melt the butter in a saucepan and let cool. In a bowl, combine the rest of the ingredients and add the cooled melted butter. Pour into the casserole.
3. Place the casserole in a pan filled with 1½ inches of hot water. Bake until set, about 1½ hours.

Sagaponack Corn Bread Casserole

*W*hen we first rented a house on Hedges Lane in Sagaponack—a tiny area wedged in between East Hampton and Bridgehampton on the South Fork of Long Island—we used to get our mail and our basic kitchen supplies at the Sagaponack General Store. For fifteen years after that we went to Europe each summer, but eventually we returned to the bucolic charm of the Hamptons.

Among many changes, one of the most noticeable was the metamorphosis of the Sagaponack General Store. It still functions as the town post office and general store, but owners Donald and Mary Spellman have made it much more. The Sagaponack General Store has become one of the most popular caterers in the Hamptons. For exhausted weekenders who would rather pay than cook, Mary turns out anything from tea sandwiches to roasted duck.

Mary's signature dish is this incredible corn bread casserole. While we don't generally use mixes and such, this casserole is so good we happily make an exception.

Makes 8 cups (16 ½-cup servings)

3 tablespoons unsalted butter	2 cups corn muffin mix (We use Flako.)
1 medium onion, chopped	
2 extra-large eggs	1½ cups sour cream
3 cups creamed corn	2½ cups grated cheddar cheese
½ cup flour	

1. Preheat the oven to 400 degrees.
2. Melt the butter in a skillet and sauté the onion until translucent.
3. In a mixing bowl combine the eggs, corn, flour, and muffin mix. Mix well. Add the sautéed onion and mix again.
4. Pour the batter into a well-greased 8 by 11-inch baking dish. Tap to make sure the batter is level, then spread the sour cream on top. Sprinkle the grated cheddar on top of the sour cream.
5. Bake for 25 minutes in the preheated oven. Reduce the temperature to 350 degrees and bake for an additional 25 minutes or until the casserole feels firm in the center.

VARIATION: Add slices of spicy sausage or crisp, crumbled bacon to the batter. If you are making this in the summer add the kernels cut from one fresh ear of corn.

ADVANCE PREPARATION: Can be prepared 2 days ahead. Cover and refrigerate. Bring to room temperature before reheating. This casserole also freezes well.

Corn Fritters

$\mathcal{I}$f the corn you are using is very fresh and sweet, cut down slightly on the sugar. As a variation, substitute brown sugar, honey, or maple syrup for the sugar.

Because this can be a time-consuming procedure, make only for a small group or freeze a batch in advance and reheat for 10 minutes at 425 degrees.

Makes about 25

3 cups fresh or frozen corn
    kernels
2 tablespoons unsalted butter
2 tablespoons sugar
2 eggs, beaten
2 tablespoons heavy cream
¼ cup all-purpose flour
¼ cup matzo meal or unsalted
    cracker crumbs

1 teaspoon baking powder
¼ teaspoon cayenne
1½ tablespoons chopped fresh
    chives
1¼ teaspoons salt
Freshly ground pepper
Corn oil

1. Cook the corn in a saucepan of boiling water until tender, about 5 minutes. Drain well. Melt the butter in a heavy skillet and sauté the corn, stirring frequently, for 3 minutes. Add the sugar and stir for another 2 minutes. Transfer the corn to a small bowl, using a slotted spoon. Set aside.

2. Combine the eggs, cream, flour, matzo meal, baking powder, cayenne, chives, salt, and pepper in a medium-size bowl. Fold in the corn and stir to distribute the kernels throughout the batter.

3. Fill a heavy skillet with corn oil to a depth of 1 inch. Warm over medium heat until a corn kernel dropped into the oil sizzles and floats to the top. With a spoon, scoop heaping tablespoons of the batter and slide them gently into the oil. As the fritters brown on the bottom, turn them with tongs. When golden brown all over, remove the fritters and drain them on paper towels.

ADVANCE PREPARATION: These fritters can be prepared 5 hours ahead. Cool. Place them on a cookie sheet and cover with plastic wrap; let stand at room temperature. Before serving, remove the plastic and bake the fritters in a 350-degree oven until heated through.

Stuffed Acorn Squash

Serves 8

4 acorn squash
Salt
½ butternut squash (about
   1 pound), peeled and cut in
   ¼-inch dice
2 cups whole cranberries

3 tablespoons lingonberry
   preserves (We use Felix Wild
   Lingonberries in Sugar. If you
   can't find this product,
   substitute raspberry
   preserves.)
1 tablespoon honey
2 tablespoons unsalted butter

1. Preheat the oven to 350 degrees. Cut the acorn squash into halves lengthwise. With a spoon scrape out the seeds and fibers. Put halves, face up, into one or more shallow baking dishes and add ¼ inch hot water. Bake for 30 minutes, or until tender.

2. Meanwhile blanch the butternut squash in boiling salted water for 3 minutes. Strain and reserve. In another pot, blanch the cranberries until the berries start to pop, about 5 minutes. Strain and combine with the butternut squash.

3. In a small saucepan, heat the lingonberries and the honey until they bubble. Add the butter. When it melts, add the cranberry-squash mixture and stir to combine—gently so as not to mash the berries. Spoon the filling into the cooked acorn squash.

4. Return the stuffed squash to the oven for 15 minutes. Serve immediately.

ADVANCE PREPARATION: Can be prepared 1 day ahead through step 3. Cover and refrigerate. Bring to room temperature before heating in a 350-degree oven for 15 minutes.

Puréed Butternut Squash

*T*his is extremely easy. It can be made ahead and can be the base for a splendid soup (see page 25).

Makes 12 cups (16 ¾-cup servings)

4 medium butternut squash
    (about 1½ pounds each)
Olive oil
4 cloves garlic, unpeeled

4 tablespoons maple syrup
4 tablespoons unsalted butter
Salt and freshly ground pepper

1. Preheat the oven to 350 degrees. With a sharp knife cut off the stem and split each squash in half from top to bottom. With a pastry brush, paint the cut side of each half with a light coating of olive oil. Place the squash, cut side down, in a roasting pan containing 1 cup of water. Sprinkle the unpeeled garlic cloves around the pan. Bake in the oven for 1 hour, or until the squash is quite soft.

2. When the squash are done, scoop out their seeds and discard. With a spoon, scoop the pulp into the bowl of a food processor or an electric mixer. Squeeze the garlic cloves out of their skins into the squash. Add the maple syrup and butter, and purée. Add salt and pepper to taste, and serve.

ADVANCE PREPARATION: Can be prepared 2 days ahead. Cover and refrigerate. Bring to room temperature before reheating in the top of a double boiler.

Gratin of Squash, Leeks, and Rice

*O*ne of our best friends and favorite cooks is Diane Rossen Worthington. This recipe appears in her excellent book, *The Taste of Summer,* but it works just fine at Thanksgiving.

We have made this many times and adapted it to our cooking style. The only substantive change that has crept into our method is to use Arborio rice instead of long-grain rice.

Makes 9 cups (18 ½-cup servings)

2½ pounds yellow squash and
   green zucchini, grated
1½ teaspoons salt
½ cup Arborio rice
¼ cup olive oil
3 medium leeks, well-cleaned
   white and light green parts
   only, finely chopped (about
   3 cups)

2 medium garlic cloves, minced
2 tablespoons finely chopped
   fresh Italian parsley
2 tablespoons flour
2 cups half-and-half
¾ cup grated Parmesan cheese
¼ teaspoon freshly ground
   pepper

1. Place the grated squash in a colander set over a bowl and add 1 teaspoon salt, tossing to distribute evenly. Allow the juices to drain for 15 to 30 minutes.

2. Squeeze the squash in handfuls or wring it out in a clean dish towel over the bowl to collect the juices. Reserve the juices and dry the squash carefully on paper towels.

3. In a medium saucepan bring 1½ cups of water to a boil and add the rice. Simmer for 10 minutes. Drain and reserve.

4. In a 10-inch ovenproof skillet, heat 1 tablespoon olive oil over medium-high heat. Sauté the leeks until slightly soft, about 5 minutes.

5. Add the remaining olive oil and sauté the shredded squash over medium-high heat until almost tender and all liquid is evaporated, about 4 minutes. Add the garlic and parsley. Sauté for 1 minute.

6. Sprinkle with the flour and stir over medium heat, using a pasta fork, for 2 minutes. Remove from the heat, add the partially cooked rice, ½ cup half-and-half, and ¼ cup vegetable liquid, and stir to combine. Continue cooking, stirring constantly until slightly thickened, about 3 minutes.

7. Continue adding the cream, ½ cup at a time, cooking until thickening begins to occur. After the last of the half-and-half has been added, stir in all but 2 tablespoons of the Parmesan. Add the remaining salt and the pepper.

8. Preheat the oven to 425 degrees. Sprinkle the remaining cheese on top of the dish. Bake until browned and bubbling, about 25 minutes.

ADVANCE PREPARATION: Can be prepared 1 day ahead through step 7. Cover and refrigerate. Bring to room temperature before baking in 425-degree oven.

Baked Pumpkins
with Mascarpone and Sage

*T*his recipe by Heidi Insalata Krahling is an adaptation of a classic French dish in which soup is cooked inside a small pumpkin. Try to get small pumpkins, 6 to 8 inches across, and wider than they are high.

This is a stylish and rather dramatic dish that probably would be best at a small Thanksgiving dinner.

Serves 8

8 miniature pumpkins	½ teaspoon freshly ground
1 pound mascarpone cheese	pepper
3 eggs	Fresh sage leaves
1 teaspoon sugar	¾ cup roasted, skinned, and
½ teaspoon salt	chopped hazelnuts

1. Preheat the oven to 350 degrees.

2. With a sharp knife, carefully cut out a lid in each pumpkin. Reserve the lids. Scoop out the seeds and discard. In a shallow baking pan fitted with a wire rack, place the pumpkins and their lids on the rack upside down. Fill the pan with ¼ inch water and bake pumpkins about 30 minutes, or until they are almost cooked but still firm. Let cool to room temperature.

3. Meanwhile, in a bowl whisk the mascarpone, eggs, sugar, salt, and pepper until smooth. Fill the pumpkins three-fourths full, alternating 1 or 2 sage leaves, a spoonful of cheese mixture, and a sprinkling of chopped hazelnuts.

4. Fit the lids back on top. Place the pumpkins back on the rack, and bake until the mascarpone is set—about 20 minutes. Serve hot.

Brussels Sprouts with
Maple-Mustard Sauce

*T*he key to this dish is not to overcook the sprouts and to make sure that each and every one of them is well coated with the sauce. This is an eclectic combination of flavors that comes together to make a delectable dish—one that has become quite popular at our house.

Makes 5 cups (10 ½-cup servings)

4 cups (2 pounds) brussels
   sprouts
2 tablespoons champagne
   vinegar
2 tablespoons balsamic vinegar
2 tablespoons maple syrup
2 tablespoons Dijon mustard
1 tablespoon coarse-grain
   mustard

½ teaspoon salt
½ teaspoon freshly ground
   pepper
⅛ teaspoon freshly grated
   nutmeg
½ cup extra-virgin olive oil

1. Trim the brussels sprouts by cutting an X in the stalk end and removing the bitter outer leaves. Drop the sprouts into a large pot containing 7 to 8 quarts of rapidly boiling water. Add 2 teaspoons of salt and bring the water back to a boil. Reduce the heat and simmer slowly for 5 minutes. Remove from the heat and drain thoroughly, letting the sprouts stand for a few minutes.

2. While the sprouts are cooking, mix the vinegars, syrup, mustards, salt, pepper, and nutmeg. Whisk thoroughly. Slowly add oil, a drop or two at a time, then in a thin, steady stream. The mixture will get thicker and lighter in color.

3. Add the brussels sprouts to the bowl containing the sauce. Toss well to coat each sprout. Serve at room temperature.

ADVANCE PREPARATION: Can be made 1 day in advance through step 2. Cover and refrigerate. Bring to room temperature and assemble 2 hours before serving.

Marinated Brussels Sprouts with Pomegranate Seeds and Walnuts

*L*et's face it, brussels sprouts are not the world's most popular vegetable. Some people—especially kids—cringe at the thought of them. But much of the bad reputation these small members of the cabbage family have earned is more a result of poor cooking than anything intrinsically wrong with the vegetable itself.

When not overcooked, brussels sprouts have a charming, subtle flavor. This recipe preserves that flavor and adds the tang of vinegar, the richness of walnuts, and the lovely perfume of pomegranate.

Dealing with the pomegranate takes some skill. The edible seeds, encased in juicy outer flesh, are mounted on a network of waxy membranes. The pomegranate has to be carefully opened and the seeds cautiously removed. The juice can stain, so take steps to protect yourself and your kitchen.

Start by cutting off the blossom end of the fruit and then carefully score the outer skin in quarters, from blossom end to stem. Do not cut into the interior of the fruit; break it carefully to reveal the seeds inside. Separate into quarters, gently remove the seeds, and place them in a bowl.

Makes 6 cups (12 ½-cup servings)

4 cups (2 pounds) brussels sprouts	½ teaspoon salt
1 cup coarsely chopped walnuts	Freshly ground pepper
4 tablespoons raspberry or red wine vinegar	½ cup walnut oil
	The seeds of 1 pomegranate

1. Trim the brussels sprouts by cutting an X in the stalk end and removing the bitter outer leaves. Drop the sprouts into a large pot containing 7 to 8 quarts of rapidly boiling water. Add 1 tablespoon of salt and bring the water back to a boil. Reduce the heat and simmer slowly for 5 minutes. Remove from heat and drain. Rinse the sprouts quickly with cold water to stop the cooking. (If you prefer, you may steam the sprouts for 8 minutes.) Cool.

2. Toast the chopped walnuts in a single layer on a foil-lined cookie sheet for 10 minutes in a 350-degree oven. Cool and reserve.

3. In a small bowl, combine the vinegar, salt, and pepper. Beat rapidly with a wire whisk while adding the walnut oil in a slow, steady stream.

4. When the brussels sprouts are at room temperature, pour the vinaigrette over them and toss to coat thoroughly. Sprinkle the walnuts over the sprouts. Marinate at room temperature for at least 2 hours. When ready to serve, sprinkle the pomegranate seeds decoratively over the brussels sprouts.

ADVANCE PREPARATION: Can be made 1 day ahead through step 3 and refrigerated. The dish can be assembled the morning of Thanksgiving and served at room temperature.

Sweet and Sour Red Cabbage

Although good with turkey, this is really a perfect accompaniment to goose.

Makes 6 cups (12 ½-cup servings)

4 tablespoons goose fat or
    unsalted butter
1 onion, thinly sliced
6 whole cloves
6 juniper berries
½ cup balsamic vinegar
¼ cup cider vinegar
2 tablespoons golden brown
    sugar

One 2-pound head red cabbage,
    finely shredded
2 tablespoons dark unsulfured
    molasses
Salt and freshly ground pepper
Lemon juice (optional)

1. Melt the fat or butter in a large skillet and sauté the onion until it is translucent, about 5 minutes. Add cloves, juniper berries, vinegars, and sugar. Bring to a boil, stirring constantly. Mix in cabbage. Reduce to a simmer, cover, and cook until cabbage is very tender and almost no liquid remains in the skillet, about 40 minutes.

2. Add molasses and season to taste with salt and pepper. For a more pungent flavor, add lemon juice to taste.

ADVANCE PREPARATION: Can be made 1 day ahead. Cover and refrigerate. Rewarm over low heat.

The Ultimate Mashed Potatoes

*W*hile our son Toby was at boarding school, he would bring his friend Barrett home for Thanksgiving. For four years Barrett was at our holiday table mainly because of these wonderful, easy-to-make mashed potatoes. We usually had to double this recipe to accommodate Barrett's appetite. These potatoes make a perfect vehicle for gravy.

In the unlikely event there are some of these left over, take a look at the Mashed Potato Pancakes on page 197.

Makes 9 cups (12 ¾-cup servings)

4 pounds medium potatoes
8 tablespoons (1 stick) unsalted
   butter

½ cup heavy cream
1 tablespoon salt
6 tablespoons chopped chives

1. Peel the potatoes and drop them into a large pot of boiling water. Boil over medium heat for 25 minutes. Drain into a colander and return to the pan. Shake over high heat to remove excess moisture.

2. Put the potatoes into the bowl of an electric mixer fitted with a paddle. Mix at slow speed. Add the butter and then the cream and salt. If serving immediately, fold the chives into the potatoes, saving some to sprinkle on the top.

VARIATIONS: Sauté the peeled cloves from one head of garlic (about 15) in the butter. Simmer for 20 minutes, making sure that the garlic does not brown. When the garlic is soft, purée it with the butter and mix it into the potatoes.

For fluffier mashed potatoes, put cooked potatoes through a ricer instead of using the mixer.

Mashed Potatoes and Celery Root

Celery root adds deep flavor complexity to the usual mashed potatoes. We thought the kids would riot when we served this, but they actually liked it.

If you have leftovers, this works well in the Mashed Potato Pancakes recipe (see page 197).

Makes 12 cups (16 ¾-cup servings)

2 pounds celery root	1 cup half-and-half
4 pounds potatoes	2 teaspoons salt
½ pound (2 sticks) unsalted butter	Freshly ground white pepper

1. Peel the celery root and cut into ¾-inch cubes. Place in a bowl with cold water to cover and reserve.

2. Put about 2 quarts of water into a medium-size pot. Peel the potatoes and cut them into ¾-inch cubes. As you finish each potato, drop the cubes into the pot. When you have finished, adjust the amount of water so that the potatoes are covered by 2 inches of water. Add 1 teaspoon salt and bring to a boil.

3. Boil the potatoes for 5 minutes, then add the drained celery root. Reduce the heat, cover, and simmer for 12 minutes, or until tender. Drain.

4. Place the vegetables in a food processor fitted with the metal blade and purée for a few seconds, or use a potato ricer. Add the butter, half-and-half, the 2 teaspoons salt, and pepper to taste, then process for a few more seconds.

5. Return the potatoes and celery root to the pot and stir over medium heat. Serve immediately.

Classic Candied Yams

Serves 10

5 yams (about 2½ pounds),
   scrubbed
2 tablespoons unsalted butter
¼ cup firmly packed brown
   sugar

1 teaspoon freshly grated
   gingerroot
1 teaspoon lemon juice

1. Bring 2 cups of water to a rolling boil in the bottom of a large saucepan. Put the yams in a steamer and cover the pot. Cook over moderate heat for 30 minutes, or until a fork can pierce the yams easily.

2. Remove the yams from the steamer and allow to cool while you make the glaze.

3. In a saucepan, melt the butter over medium-low heat and add brown sugar. Stir until dissolved. Add the ginger, simmer for 1 minute, then add the lemon juice.

4. Butter an ovenproof baking dish 7 by 11 by 1½ inches. Peel the yams and slice them in half, lengthwise. Place them flat side down in the dish, and cover with the glaze.

5. Preheat the oven to 350 degrees. Bake for 15 minutes. Serve.

ADVANCE PREPARATION: Can be prepared 1 day ahead through step 4. When ready to serve, remove from the refrigerator and let the dish come to room temperature, then bake at 350 degrees for 15 minutes, or until warmed through.

Maddie's Praline Sweet Potatoes

*M*addie Katz has been making and refining this luscious recipe for nearly thirty years. It is a crowd pleaser and, although it is finished with sugar, it does a good job of showcasing the true sweet potato flavor. The Orange Sauce gives the dish an additional subtlety that is quite appealing. If desired, though, the potatoes can be served without the sauce.

Makes 6 cups (12 ½-cup servings)

4 sweet potatoes	2 teaspoons salt, or to taste
2 eggs	½ cup pecan halves
½ cup firmly packed dark brown sugar	Orange Sauce (see below)
6 tablespoons unsalted butter, melted	

1. Cut a slit in each potato, place on a baking sheet, and bake at 350 degrees for 1 hour, or until soft. Leave the oven on.

2. When done, scoop out the sweet potato pulp and place in a bowl. With a wooden spoon, beat in the 2 eggs, ¼ cup sugar, 2 tablespoons melted butter, and the salt. Pour the mixture into a 2-quart casserole. Arrange the pecan halves on the top in a neat design. Sprinkle with the remaining ¼ cup sugar and drizzle with the remaining butter.

3. Bake for 20 minutes, or until heated through. To complete the dish, place under a hot broiler for 30 seconds to melt the sugar. Serve immediately accompanied by Orange Sauce.

Orange Sauce

Makes 1½ cups

⅓ cup granulated sugar	1 tablespoon freshly squeezed lemon juice
1 tablespoon cornstarch	2 tablespoons unsalted butter
Pinch of salt	1 tablespoon Cointreau, or other orange liqueur
1 teaspoon grated orange zest	3 dashes bitters
1 cup orange juice, preferably freshly squeezed	

1. Combine the sugar, cornstarch, and salt in a saucepan. Add the orange zest, and orange and lemon juices. Stir over medium heat until sauce coats the back of a spoon.

2. Remove from the heat and stir in butter, Cointreau, and the bitters.

ADVANCE PREPARATION: The casserole can be prepared 1 day ahead through step 2. Cover and refrigerate. Bring the casserole to room temperature before reheating in a 350-degree oven. The sauce can be prepared 2 days ahead. Cover tightly and refrigerate. Reheat gently before serving.

Caitlin's Potatoes

$\mathcal{T}$his is a dazzling, elegant, and extremely simple adaptation of the famous French *Pommes Anna,* the layered potato pancake that has become a classic. We named it for our eldest daughter.

Serves 8

8 tablespoons (1 stick) unsalted butter, melted	1 apple, thinly sliced
5 medium sweet potatoes, peeled	2 tablespoons maple syrup
	Salt and freshly ground pepper

1. Preheat the oven to 400 degrees. Thinly slice the potatoes by hand or use the 3 mm food processor blade. Butter a 9-inch pie pan and arrange a neat layer of overlapped sweet potato slices in it. Dribble a little melted butter over the potatoes. Place a layer of sliced apple, not overlapped, on top of the potatoes. Sprinkle with butter, maple syrup, salt, and pepper.

2. Continue layering the ingredients until the pie plate is filled, finishing with maple syrup, salt, and pepper. (All the potatoes should be used up.)

3. Cover the top with foil and a lid. Bake in the preheated oven for 45 minutes. Remove the lid and the foil and bake until the top is golden, about 15 minutes. Be careful not to overcook.

5. Remove the pan from the oven and let cool for 10 minutes. Invert onto a large round platter and, with the gentle proddings of a narrow spatula, let the crisp pancake drop onto the platter. Serve hot, cut into wedges with a pie knife.

ADVANCE PREPARATION: Can be assembled through step 2 as much as 6 hours ahead. Cover and refrigerate.

Mashed Sweet Potatoes

Makes 5 cups (10 ½-cup servings)

5 sweet potatoes (about 2½ pounds)

4 tablespoons unsalted butter, cut in pieces

¼ cup heavy cream

½ teaspoon freshly grated nutmeg

½ teaspoon freshly ground white pepper

Salt

1 tablespoon chopped fresh parsley

1. Peel the sweet potatoes and place them in a pot. Cover with lightly salted water and place over medium heat. Boil until a fork pierces the potatoes without resistance—about 20 minutes. Drain.

2. At this point, you can mash the potatoes with a potato ricer, or transfer them to a food processor fitted with the metal blade. In either case, alternately add the butter and the cream while beating or processing.

3. When smooth, add the seasonings, garnish with chopped parsley, and serve immediately.

NOTE: If you have leftovers, these potatoes work very nicely in the Mashed Potato Pancakes (page 197).

ADVANCE PREPARATION: Can be prepared 2 days ahead. Cover and refrigerate. Store the parsley separately. Bring to room temperature before reheating in the top of a double boiler.

Wild Rice Ragout

*T*his recipe was suggested by Heidi Insalata Krahling, one of California's most talented young cooks. She is chef at Smith Ranch in San Rafael. Heidi Insalata Krahling's wild rice ragout is very rich and quite extraordinary. It is best served at a smaller, more sophisticated Thanksgiving. It goes beautifully with duck or goose and works well as a stuffing.

Makes 5 cups (10 ½-cup servings)

1½ cups wild rice
3 cloves garlic, peeled
2 bay leaves
5 cups Chicken Stock (see page 77)
2 tablespoons unsalted butter
4 shallots, finely minced
1 large or 2 small heads fennel, thinly sliced
1 tablespoon toasted and ground fennel seed

½ cup brandy
2 cups rich condensed poultry (squab or duck) stock
½ cup orange juice
2 tablespoons chopped fresh chives
¼ cup fresh tarragon leaves, chopped
1 cup chestnuts, preferably freshly roasted and peeled
Salt and freshly ground pepper

COMPOUND BUTTER

6 tablespoons unsalted butter, softened
Grated zest of 1 orange

2 shallots, roasted until golden, then chopped

1. Place the wild rice, garlic, bay leaves, and stock in a saucepan, and bring to a boil over medium heat. Reduce heat to low and simmer until the rice is tender. (Different wild rice brands seem to have different cooking times. Taste a few grains of the rice to make sure that it is soft enough.) Drain the liquid and set the rice aside. Discard the garlic and bay leaves.

2. Melt the 2 tablespoons butter in a sauté pan. Sauté the shallots until softened. Add the sliced fennel and continue to sauté for about 1 minute. Add the ground fennel seed and sauté for 30 seconds more. Deglaze the pan with brandy.

3. Add the rich stock and the orange juice, and reduce the liquid by half. Add the reserved wild rice, the chives, tarragon, chestnuts, and salt and pepper to taste. Stir to mix.

4. Make the compound butter by combining the softened butter, the orange zest, and the chopped roasted shallots. Over low heat, swirl the compound butter into the rice. Season to taste.

ADVANCE PREPARATION: Can be prepared 1 day in advance. Cover and refrigerate. Bring to room temperature before warming in the top of a double boiler.

Spicy Rice

*I*f you're weary of mashed potatoes or candied yams, this is a dazzling alternative. Earthy, rich, and complex in flavor, this rice is a worthy accompaniment to turkey.

Makes 5 cups (10 ½-cup servings)

2 tablespoons vegetable oil	½ cup chopped red onion
2 shallots, minced	1 teaspoon salt
3 cloves garlic, minced	¼ teaspoon cayenne
2 cups long-grain rice	2 tablespoons chopped fresh
3 cups Chicken Stock (see	parsley
page 77)	

1. In a saucepan, heat the oil over medium-high heat and add the shallots and garlic. Sauté until lightly browned. Remove from the heat and reserve.

2. Rinse the rice quickly and drain for 10 minutes. Add the rice to the saucepan and sauté over medium-high heat for 5 minutes. Add the stock and cover, cook for 7 minutes, stirring only twice. The stock should be completely absorbed.

3. Reduce the heat to low. Add the red onion and cook for 10 minutes longer. Stir in salt and cayenne. Garnish with parsley and serve.

ADVANCE PREPARATION: Can be prepared 4 hours ahead. Cover and store at room temperature. Reheat in the top of a double boiler.

Corn and Tomato Salad with Mustard-Cumin Vinaigrette

*T*his mellow salad brings some new flavors to the Thanksgiving table. The crisp combination of corn, tomatoes, and cumin is a charming contrast to the heavy, rich foods of the season. We also love this for luncheons during the holiday weekend.

Makes 6 cups (8 ¾-cup servings)

4 cups frozen or fresh corn (cut from 8 ears)
1¼ cups chopped red onions
12 cherry tomatoes, quartered
½ cup chopped fresh parsley
1½ teaspoons cumin

1 tablespoon Dijon mustard
1 tablespoon balsamic vinegar
2 tablespoons red wine vinegar
¾ cup extra-virgin olive oil
½ teaspoon salt
Freshly ground pepper

1. If you are using fresh corn, shuck it partially (let a few of the outer leaves remain), and boil for 8 minutes in a large pot of salted water. Remove from the water and let cool. (You can cook the corn well in advance and refrigerate it until ready to use.) Slice the kernels from each ear. If you are using frozen corn, use the loose kind packed in plastic bags. Allow the corn to defrost.

2. In a large bowl, combine the corn, onions, tomatoes, and parsley. Stir.

3. Combine the remaining ingredients in a screw-top jar or small bowl. Shake vigorously or stir to emulsify.

4. Pour the vinaigrette over the corn mixture and stir to combine. Serve or refrigerate until ready to use. This salad will keep for several days in the refrigerator.

VARIATION: A nontraditional but appealing variation is to add ½ cup of crumbled feta cheese to the salad.

ADVANCE PREPARATION: Can be prepared 2 days ahead, but don't add the tomatoes until ready to serve. Cover and refrigerate.

Condiments

*C*ondiments are a northern European invention. We'd like to think they were created to liven up food that was traditionally bland. Because the colonists who participated in the early Thanksgivings were English, condiments became an important part of the holiday festival and, since they were readily available, cranberries became the condiment of choice.

Cranberries are small, extremely sour berries that grow in sea-level peat bogs, particularly in the New England areas where the Pilgrims settled. They are similar to lingonberries, which are used in Northern Europe as an accompaniment. Because they are so sour, cranberries must be combined with sugar to become palatable. Thus they are ideal for making sweet relishes and sauces.

Cranberries are one of only three native North American fruits (Concord grapes and blueberries are the other two). In fact, long before the settlers arrived in 1620, North American Indians were already combining dried venison with suet and cranberries to make pemmican—a long-lasting convenience food.

The Indians had other uses for cranberries. In addition to their culinary applications, they employed cranberries as dye and they believed that the cranberry had special medicinal properties. Indian women used the bright red juice to color blankets and rugs, and poultices for cleansing infections were brewed from whole cranberries.

In the nineteenth century, American sailors went to sea with barrels of cranberries. The berries were for vitamin C, needed to ward off scurvy (English sailors used limes for the same purpose, thus the nickname *limey).*

The cranberry was named by the colonists. Indians had called it *sassananesh* and *ibimi,* but the Pilgrims thought the bright berry blossom looked like the head of a crane, so they called them *craneberries,* which was eventually contracted to its present form.

Cranberries are grown mainly in bogs or marshes in eastern Massachusetts and Rhode Island. They can also be found in New Jersey, Wisconsin, and along the Pacific coast in Oregon, Washington, and British Columbia.

Cranberry bogs are peat-based swamps that have been drained and topped with a layer of sand. This acid environment is ideal for the trailing vines on which the berries grow. It takes 3 to 5 years for a new plantation to bear a commercial crop, but if care is taken to guard against frost damage, cranberry vines can bear indefinitely. There are some producing bogs that are over one hundred years old.

The vines blossom in the latter part of June or early July and the ripe berries are harvested in September and October. In the past cranberries were painstakingly picked by hand; now they are wet-harvested by flooding the beds. Mechanical harvesters cause the ripe berries to float to the surface where they are scooped up and boxed.

Most cranberries are then delivered to Ocean Spray, a grower cooperative that was formed in 1930. Ocean Spray packages and freezes millions of pounds of the sour little berries. The company also introduced a line of cranberry drinks in 1967 that have become extremely successful.

Fresh cranberries are low in calories. An uncooked half cup has only 25 calories and provides more than 10 percent of the recommended daily allowance of vitamin C.

If you plan to use cranberries at times of the year other than Thanksgiving, buy them in the autumn and freeze; they will keep very well for nine months in the freezer. When using frozen berries, do not thaw.

ADVANCE PREPARATION

The recipes that follow can be made a week or two before Thanksgiving. They should be cooled, jarred, and refrigerated. Most of them actually improve with age. If you want to keep them longer than three weeks, can them in sterilized, airtight jars. In this form, they will keep for several months; they make excellent gifts.

Cranberry Relish

Several years ago Andy was the judge at the National Cranberry Cook-off held in Los Angeles. The winning recipe was for cranberry-cherry relish. The lady who created it, Mrs. Helen Lacina of Grinnell, Iowa, won $1,000 and an engraved silver trophy for her creative efforts.

We have adapted this recipe over the years and it has become a tradition at the Blue house. We found the canned cherries to be a problem so we eliminated them. (The recipe called for 1 cup of pitted cherries, and only the canned version is available at Thanksgiving time. If you were to make this relish during cherry season, by all means add 1 cup of fresh pitted cherries to the blend or use dried cherries, if you can get them.)

Each year Andy gives the recipe on his WCBS radio show in New York and more than 1,000 people write in for a printed copy of it.

This relish can be made well ahead of the Thanksgiving dinner. It will keep nicely in the refrigerator for 2 to 3 weeks, or it can be frozen in plastic containers. It is quite good with ham, chicken, or pork. If you are a guest at someone else's home for Thanksgiving dinner, this relish makes a fine house present.

Makes 6 cups

1 lemon, quartered and seeded	½ cup white vinegar
1 orange, quartered and seeded	½ teaspoon ground cinnamon
1½ cups fresh or frozen whole cranberries	½ teaspoon ground cloves
2 cups dark brown sugar	½ teaspoon freshly grated nutmeg
1½ cups raisins	½ cinnamon stick

Cut the lemon and orange into pieces no bigger than ½ inch. Place them in a large saucepan with all the other ingredients. Bring the mixture to a boil over medium heat, reduce the heat, and simmer for 15 minutes. Remove the cinnamon stick. Cool and refrigerate.

Uncooked Cranberry Relish

*T*his classic condiment offers holiday diners a tangy contrast to cooked cranberry sauce.

Makes 3 cups

1 orange
One 12-ounce package (3 cups)
   fresh or frozen cranberries

1 cup sugar

1. With a sharp knife or vegetable peeler remove the outer skin of the orange. Inspect the skin for traces of pith, the bitter white inner skin, and cut off any that you find. Reserve the skin. Remove and discard the white pith from the orange and slice the fruit into sections, cutting off the separating membranes. Remove the seeds.

2. Put the orange slices, the orange skin, and the cranberries into the bowl of a food processor fitted with the metal blade. Pulse 4 or 5 times, or until the fruit is evenly chopped. Put the chopped fruit into a bowl or glass container. Stir in the sugar until dissolved. Refrigerate.

NOTE: This relish, because it is uncooked, will not last as long as some of the other cranberry condiments. Give it a week or two at the most.

VARIATION: Add ½ cup chopped walnuts and pulse with the other ingredients.

Traditional Cranberry Sauce

The traditional sauce—cranberries and sugar—is what most children expect and love. We like to offer a selection of condiments at the Blue holiday table, and this one is usually among them.

We generally serve this sauce along with one or two other condiments. If this is the only one you serve for a party of 8 or more, double the recipe.

Makes 2½ cups

1 cup water	One 12-ounce package (3 cups)
1 cup sugar	fresh or frozen cranberries

1. Combine the water and sugar in a saucepan. Bring to a boil over medium heat, stirring to dissolve the sugar. Add the cranberries, bring to a full boil again, and lower the heat to a simmer. Cook until the cranberry skins begin to pop.
2. Cool completely at room temperature and refrigerate.

VARIATION: Use cranberry juice cocktail instead of water, or try one of the cranberry juice combinations—Cran-Apple, Cran-Raspberry, etc.

Another idea is to add 1 or 2 teaspoons grated orange rind when adding the cranberries.

Cranberry Chutney

This easy-to-make spicy condiment is the brainchild of Susan Friedland, our editor. It not only goes with turkey, it can be used throughout the year with chicken, meatloaf, ribs, or anything else you can think of.

Makes about 1 quart

1 pound cranberries	¾ cup water
Thinly sliced peel of 1 lemon	1 teaspoon salt
1 cup brown sugar	1 teaspoon dry mustard
½ cup raisins	Cayenne
½ cup white vinegar	⅔ cup ginger preserves
1 large onion, sliced	

1. In a large saucepan, combine all ingredients except the ginger preserves. Cook over moderate heat until the mixture thickens and the cranberries pop, 30 to 45 minutes.

2. Remove the saucepan from the heat and stir in the ginger preserves. When the mixture cools, transfer to covered jars and refrigerate. The chutney will keep for months.

Cranberry Cassis Conserve

$\mathcal{T}$his is a bright, fruity, condiment with a few interesting flavor twists. It will keep well in the refrigerator for several weeks, or it can be frozen for much longer. You might use the excess for gifts or, if there's just too much, you can cut the recipe in half.

Makes 9 cups

1 thin-skinned juice orange	¼ teaspoon ground cinnamon
1 Granny Smith or other firm, tart apple, peeled, cored, and finely minced	¼ teaspoon almond extract
	4 cups (1 pound) cranberries, fresh or frozen
2 cups firmly packed dark brown sugar	1 tablespoon honey
½ cup raspberry vinegar	½ teaspoon lemon juice
½ cup dried currants	2 tablespoons crème de cassis
1 teaspoon chopped crystallized ginger	

1. Cut the orange into chunks. In a food processor fitted with the metal blade, chop the orange to a coarse meal texture. Stir in the apple.

2. In a saucepan, combine sugar and vinegar. Over moderate heat, stir to dissolve the sugar. Bring the mixture to a boil and let it bubble for 5 minutes, or until it is a syrupy consistency. Add currants, ginger, cinnamon, and almond extract. Simmer 5 more minutes. Add the cranberries and continue cooking for about another 5 minutes. Remove from the heat when the fruit begins to pop.

3. Add the orange mixture, honey, lemon juice, and cassis. Toss thoroughly to blend. Store in glass containers.

VARIATION: Add ½ cup toasted, slivered almonds and omit the cassis.

Cranberry Jelly

*T*his is a concentrated and intensely flavored natural jelly. Instead of using a jar or other container in step 3, a mold can be used. This makes for a decorative presentation at the holiday table.

Makes 1 cup

Two 12-ounce packages (6 cups)   3 cups sparkling apple cider
  fresh or frozen cranberries   1 cup sugar

1. In a 3-quart saucepan, combine all ingredients and bring to a boil, stirring to mix thoroughly. Reduce the heat to low and simmer for 1 hour.
2. Line a fine sieve with a double layer of well-rinsed cheesecloth and place over a 2-quart saucepan. Strain the mixture using the back of a ladle to squeeze the juice from the solids. Gather the corners of the cloth and twist hard to extract all the liquid. Discard the solids.
3. Over medium heat, bring the liquid to a boil. Decrease the heat to low, and simmer to reduce the liquid to 1 cup. Pour into a sterile jar or decorative 1-cup mold, cover, cool, and chill.

VARIATION: The juice and zest of one orange can be added at step 3 to make a cranberry-orange jelly. Add two cinnamon sticks (remove at the end of step 3) to add a flavor nuance.

Cranberry Vinegar

*T*his flavored vinegar is useful in many holiday recipes (substitute it anywhere berry vinegar is called for). It adds a unique Thanksgiving character to many dishes.

Makes 3 cups

1 cup cranberries   2 cups champagne vinegar

1. Place the cranberries in a clean, lidded quart bottle. Heat the vine-

gar over moderate heat. When it comes to a boil, pour it over the cranberries.

2. Let the mixture cool and then screw on the lid. Place the jar in a sunny spot and leave it undisturbed for at least a week—preferably several weeks. (We have found the optimum time is about 5 weeks.)

NOTE: This vinegar will keep at room temperature nearly indefinitely if you strain out the berries. If you find the vinegar too tart, stir in 1 or 2 teaspoons of sugar.

Spiced Cranberry Purée

𝒯his smooth, thick, spicy, and opulently flavored condiment is excellent with turkey and also is perfect with cold meats such as pork or lamb. This sauce will keep for months in the refrigerator.

Makes about 6 cups

2 pounds (about 8 cups) cranberries, sorted and washed
3 medium onions, coarsely chopped (about 2 cups)
1 cup water
2 cups light brown sugar
½ cup red wine vinegar
½ teaspoon ground ginger
½ teaspoon ground cloves
1 teaspoon ground allspice
1 teaspoon ground cinnamon
¼ teaspoon freshly ground pepper
1 teaspoon salt

1. Put the cranberries, onions, and water into a 5-quart saucepan. Bring to a boil, cover tightly, and boil for 15 minutes. Stir the mixture twice at the end of the cooking time. The berries should have popped and the onions should be tender. Drain the water.

2. In the bowl of a food processor fitted with the metal blade, purée the berries and onions. Add the rest of the ingredients and continue to process for a few seconds.

3. Return the mixture to the saucepan. Over medium heat, bring the sauce to a boil. Remove from the heat and pack at once into 6 or 7 hot, sterilized ½-pint jars, and seal. This will ensure that the sauce will stay fresh for several months.

Ginger-Apple Preserves

This very sweet confection is popular with certain younger people in our house. Frankly, we find it a bit sugary. It does go nicely with duck and goose, however, and it's quite easy to make.

Makes about 4 cups

2 pounds crisp, firm, tart apples (Granny Smiths are perfect), peeled, cored, and coarsely chopped (about 5 cups)
½ cup coarsely chopped crystallized ginger
¼ cup freshly squeezed lemon juice
Zest of 1 lemon
4 cups sugar
½ cup water

In a saucepan, bring all the ingredients to a boil. Stir until the sugar is dissolved. Reduce heat and simmer, uncovered, for 1 hour, or until the apples are tender and the preserve is thick. Cool. Refrigerate until ready to use. This keeps for weeks in the refrigerator.

Meems' Prune Chutney

This stuff is just superb. We got the recipe from our friend Mary Powell, who inherited it from her grandmother. Mary serves it with turkey and with the wonderful marinated lamb that her son Alex makes. We make sure that there is a good supply of this magical chutney in our refrigerator at all times, in case of an emergency.

Makes about 5 cups

3½ cups pitted prunes, halved
1 cup firmly packed dark brown sugar
1 cup granulated sugar
¾ cup cider vinegar
1½ teaspoons crushed red pepper flakes
2 teaspoons mustard seed
2 large cloves garlic, thinly sliced
¼ cup thinly sliced onion
½ cup thinly sliced preserved ginger
1 cup seedless white raisins

1. Bring 2 cups of water to a boil. Place the prunes in a bowl. Pour the water over the prunes and soak overnight.

2. The next day, mix the sugars and vinegar and bring them to a boil in a saucepan over medium heat. Add all other ingredients except the prunes. Mix well. Discard the soaking water and stir in the prunes. Simmer over medium-low heat until the mixture is thickened, about 1 hour, stirring gently and frequently. Pour into ½-pint glass jars and refrigerate.

Harvest Fruit Chutney

This unusual condiment is the creation of Lois Jamart, a talented San Francisco cook. It goes well with turkey and other meats, warm or cold. It keeps for months in the refrigerator.

Makes 5 cups

½ cup raisins
¼ cup brandy
½ cup apricot preserves
½ cup cider vinegar
½ cup firmly packed dark brown sugar
2 tablespoons chopped crystallized ginger
1 teaspoon curry powder
1 cinnamon stick and 6 whole cloves, wrapped in a double thickness of cheesecloth and tied

1 lime, blanched in boiling water for 2 minutes, then seeded and chopped
1 firm pear, peeled and seeded
One 12-ounce package (3 cups) fresh or frozen cranberries
½ cup chopped walnuts

1. Soak the raisins in the brandy for 2 to 4 hours.

2. In a large saucepan, combine the preserves, vinegar, sugar, ginger, curry powder, and the seasoning bag. Stir until the sugar is dissolved.

3. Add the lime and pear. Simmer over medium heat for 10 minutes. Add the cranberries and brandy-soaked raisins. Simmer, stirring occasionally, for 25 minutes, or until thick.

4. Stir in the walnuts and discard the seasoning bag. Serve immediately or refrigerate until ready to use. Bring to room temperature before serving.

Apple and Cranberry Salad

*T*his crisp and tangy salad, suggested by Martha Kropf, offers an excellent balance to the rich and heavy foods that make up the Thanksgiving feast.

Makes 8 cups

¼ cup freshly squeezed lime juice
1 tablespoon Dijon mustard
1 teaspoon salt
Several grindings of white pepper
¾ cup extra-virgin olive oil
4 tart, crisp apples such as Granny Smiths, cored and cut into ½-inch dice

½ cup thinly sliced scallions
2 cups fresh cranberries, coarsely chopped
4 tablespoons sugar
2 bunches (about 2 cups) watercress

1. In a medium-size glass bowl combine the lime juice, mustard, salt, and pepper. Stir. While beating continuously, add the olive oil in a thin, steady stream. Add the diced apple and sliced scallion. Toss to coat all the ingredients. Cover with plastic wrap. Let stand in the refrigerator for 2 to 3 hours.

2. In another glass bowl, combine the chopped cranberries and the sugar. Stir to combine well. Cover with plastic wrap. Refrigerate for 2 hours.

3. When ready to serve, line each salad plate with well-cleaned and stemmed watercress. Top with a portion of apples and of cranberries. Serve immediately.

NOTE: If you want people to help themselves, line a salad bowl with the watercress. Place the cranberries in the center of the bowl, and arrange the apples around them.

VARIATION: Substitute diced jicama for half the apples.

Onion, Prune, and Chestnut Compote

*H*ere's a real grown-up accompaniment to soothe the more sophisticated palates while the kids are slurping down the mashed potatoes, gravy, and cranberry jelly. This dish, based on an idea by Diane Rossen Worthington, is rich and quite exquisite.

Actually we couldn't quite decide whether this is a condiment or a vegetable, so we decided it's both. In smaller quantities it is an elegant condiment; in larger amounts it is a flavorful vegetable.

Makes about 6 cups

3 tablespoons butter
1 pint pearl onions (2 cups), peeled
1½ cups veal or beef stock
1 cup port
2 cups moist prunes
2 cups whole chestnuts, roasted and peeled

½ teaspoon salt
½ teaspoon freshly ground pepper
2 teaspoons finely chopped fresh thyme (use lemon thyme, if possible), or 1 tsp. dried
Thyme sprigs for garnish

1. In a small saucepan melt 2 tablespoons butter. Add onions and sauté, rolling them on all sides to coat evenly with butter. Add 1 cup stock, bring to a boil, then reduce to a simmer. Cook until the onions are translucent and soft, about 25 minutes. Set aside.

2. In another saucepan, combine ¾ cup port, prunes, and remaining stock, and bring to a boil. Reduce heat and simmer until moderately soft, about 10 minutes. Spoon the prunes into the onions.

3. In a sauté pan, melt the remaining 1 tablespoon butter and add the chestnuts. Add the remaining port and toss chestnuts to coat and lightly glaze. Combine the chestnuts with the onions and prunes. Add salt, pepper, and chopped thyme. Garnish with thyme sprigs. Serve warm or at room temperature.

ADVANCE PREPARATION: Can be prepared 3 days ahead. Cover and refrigerate. Bring to room temperature before warming over low heat.

Kumquat-Cranberry Compote

*T*his tangy concoction can be served either hot or cold.

Makes 3 cups

1 cup fresh kumquats
½ cup dry red wine

¼ cup sugar
1 package (12 ounces)
    cranberries

1. Slice the kumquats lengthwise. Place them in a 2-quart saucepan and add the wine and sugar. Simmer over moderate heat until the sugar is dissolved and the kumquats slightly softened.

2. Stir in the cranberries and bring to a boil. Reduce heat and simmer, uncovered, for about 10 minutes, or until the berries begin to pop. Remove from the heat. Cool to room temperature and serve or cover and refrigerate.

Breads and Muffins

*T*he Thanksgiving feast does not really need bread, but there are a few that are appropriate, especially corn bread, a good accompaniment to turkey and a basis for several stuffings.

Basic Corn Bread

---

*T*his is a good, moist corn bread that is fine on its own and perfect as an ingredient in various stuffings. The recipe can be doubled. Use a 10 by 15-inch pan for a double recipe.

For stuffing purposes, this recipe makes 6½ cups when crumbled

½ cup all-purpose flour
2½ teaspoons baking powder
1 teaspoon salt
1½ tablespoons sugar
1½ cups yellow cornmeal

3 tablespoons unsalted butter,
  melted
¾ cup milk or buttermilk
1 egg

1. Preheat the oven to 425 degrees. Sift the flour, baking powder, salt, and sugar together into a large bowl. Add the cornmeal and stir with a fork to combine.

2. In a small bowl, beat the butter, milk, and egg together. Pour into the flour mixture and stir a few times to combine. Do not overbeat.

3 Pour into a well-greased 9 by 9-inch pan. Bake for 25 minutes, or until firm in the center.

Harvest Corn Sticks

*T*hese are made in well-cured, heavy cast-iron molds that are shaped like ears of corn. Traditionally each of these molds makes 7 corn sticks. This recipe makes about 40 corn sticks but since few people own 6 molds, they can be made in shifts. We recommend that you have at least 2 molds, and preferably 3. Keep the corn sticks warm and serve with plenty of soft butter.

Makes 40 corn sticks

2¾ cups all-purpose flour	3 eggs, beaten
1 cup yellow cornmeal	1 cup creamed corn
2 tablespoons baking powder	¼ cup vegetable oil
2 teaspoons salt	1½ cups half-and-half
½ cup superfine sugar	

1. Preheat oven to 425 degrees. In a bowl, combine all the dry ingredients. Form a well in the center.

2 In another bowl, mix eggs, creamed corn, vegetable oil, and half-and-half. Pour the mixture into the well, stir just to mix. The mixture will be lumpy.

3. Heat cast-iron corn stick pans in the oven for 5 minutes. Remove the pans and grease them generously with bacon fat or vegetable oil. Fill each mold three-fourths full with the corn mixture. Bake about 20 minutes, until golden brown. Serve warm.

Corn Muffins

*T*hese are plump, rich, and very delicious. Serve them warm.

Makes 12 muffins

2 cups yellow cornmeal	1 teaspoon salt
¾ cup all-purpose flour	2 eggs
2½ tablespoons sugar	1½ cups milk
2 tablespoons baking powder	½ cup shortening

1. Combine the dry ingredients in a large bowl. Add 1 egg, mix thoroughly, add the second egg, and mix again. Blend in the milk thoroughly. Add the shortening and mix again. Cover and refrigerate for at least 1 hour.

2. Preheat the oven to 350 degrees. Butter or grease the cups (2¾ inches in diameter) of a standard 12-muffin pan. Fill each cup two-thirds full of batter. Bake muffins until their tops are golden brown, about 20 minutes.

Whole Wheat Corn Bread

*T*his variation is the brainchild of Barbara Folger, who summers on Cape Cod. It works best with a stone ground cornmeal. Barbara gets her ground cornmeal from Leo Manning at Dexter's Grist Mill in Sandwich, Massachusetts.

Makes 1 7 × 1½-inch loaf

2 eggs	1 teaspoon salt
½ cup sugar	1 tablespoon baking powder
1 cup whole wheat flour	1 tablespoon unsalted butter,
1 cup all-purpose flour	melted
1 cup cornmeal	1½ cups milk

1. Preheat the oven to 425 degrees.
2. In a large bowl, beat the eggs and add the sugar. In another bowl,

sift the two flours, cornmeal, salt, and baking powder together. Add the dry ingredients to the egg mixture and stir in the milk and melted butter.

3. Pour the batter into a 7 by 11 by 1½-inch Pyrex baking dish. Bake in the preheated oven until set, about 20 minutes.

ADVANCE PREPARATION: Can be prepared 2 days ahead. Cover and store at room temperature. This corn bread also can be frozen for two months.

Martha Pearl's Buttermilk Biscuits

Martha Pearl Villas—food writer Jim Villas's mother—is perhaps the best native Southern cook we have ever met. Her fried chicken is so good that only the hot biscuits that are served alongside can compete.

We like these with Thanksgiving dinner because they are easy to make and are a perfect contrast to the richer textures and flavors of the rest of the meal. The recipe can be doubled.

Makes 20 biscuits

2 cups all-purpose flour	½ teaspoon salt
4 teaspoons baking powder	¼ cup shortening
½ teaspoon baking soda	1 cup buttermilk

1. Preheat the oven to 475 degrees.

2. Sift the dry ingredients together into a medium bowl. Add the shortening in small pieces and mix with your hands until well blended. Add the buttermilk and mix again until soft but—and this is the key—don't over-mix.

3. Turn the dough out onto a lightly floured surface and shape with your hands until smooth. Flatten the dough into a rough rectangle with a ½-inch thickness. Cut out rounds with a floured 2-inch cutter or juice glass. Place the biscuits on a baking sheet. Ball up the scraps of dough and repeat the procedure.

4. Bake the biscuits for 12 minutes, or until they are lightly browned on top.

Buttermilk-Sage Biscuits

Makes about 30 biscuits

½ cup white cornmeal
1½ cups all-purpose flour
2 teaspoons baking powder
½ teaspoon baking soda
2 tablespoons minced fresh sage,
    or 1 tablespoon crumbled
    dried

1½ teaspoons freshly ground
    pepper
½ teaspoon salt
6 tablespoons unsalted butter,
    chilled
⅔ cup buttermilk

1. Preheat the oven to 425 degrees. Grease a baking sheet.

2. In a bowl mix the cornmeal, flour, baking powder, baking soda, sage, pepper, and salt. Toss with a fork to combine. Cut the butter into the bowl and mix with a pastry blender or your fingers.

3. Add the buttermilk and stir just until the dough holds together. Do not overmix.

4. Turn the dough out onto a lightly floured surface. Knead with the heels of your hands a few times. Pat the dough to a ½-inch thickness.

5. With a 1½-inch-diameter round cutter, cut out the biscuits and place them, in a tight formation, on the baking sheet. If you have leftover dough scraps, press them together and cut out more biscuits.

6. Bake the biscuits in the preheated oven for 12 to 15 minutes, until lightly browned.

Cranberry-Orange Muffins

Makes 12 muffins

4 tablespoons unsalted butter
1¼ cups sugar
2 eggs
2 cups all-purpose flour
2 teaspoons baking powder
¼ teaspoon salt

½ cup half-and-half
Zest of 1 orange, chopped
2 cups cranberries, coarsely
    chopped
3 tablespoons orange juice

1. Preheat the oven to 350 degrees. In the bowl of a mixer, cream the butter and sugar together. Continue beating and add the eggs, one at a time.

2. Sift the dry ingredients and add to the butter-sugar mixture, alternating with the cream. Add the orange zest, cranberries, and orange juice.

3. Grease a 12-muffin tin with the softened butter. Spoon the mixture into the cups, filling them three-fourths full. Bake 35 minutes in the preheated oven, or until a toothpick or cake tester inserted in the center of a muffin comes out clean.

Popovers

*C*ommonly served with roast beef, these wonderfully crisp and airy creations are also delicious with turkey.

Makes 18 popovers

1 cup milk	2 eggs
1 cup all-purpose flour	3 tablespoons unsalted butter,
½ teaspoon salt	melted

1. Preheat the oven to 450 degrees.

2. Butter 18 muffin tins or popover cups. In the bowl of a food processor fitted with the metal blade, add the milk, flour, salt, and eggs. Process for 2 minutes.

3. Fill each muffin or popover cup one-third full and pour ½ teaspoon melted butter in the center of each.

4. Bake in preheated oven for 10 minutes, then lower the heat to 400. After 25 additional minutes, poke a small hole in each popover to let out the steam. Leave in the oven 3 minutes to crisp.

ADVANCE PREPARATION: Although popovers are best when fresh from the oven, they can be made a day ahead and reheated. Remove them from the oven before the 3-minute crisping time (step 4). Cover with foil and store at room temperature until ready to use. Then warm in a 250-degree oven for 4 minutes.

Pumpkin-Hazelnut Bread

Makes 18 ½-inch slices

1½ cups all-purpose flour
1 teaspoon baking soda
¼ teaspoon baking powder
¾ teaspoon salt
1 teaspoon ground cinnamon
¼ teaspoon freshly grated
   nutmeg

6 tablespoons butter
1⅓ cups sugar
1 cup puréed or mashed
   pumpkin
2 eggs, lightly beaten
⅓ cup milk
1 cup chopped hazelnuts

1. Preheat the oven to 350 degrees. Grease and flour a 9 by 5-inch loaf pan.

2. In a medium bowl combine the first six ingredients, and stir with a fork to incorporate.

3. In a large bowl blend the butter and sugar with a fork. Add the pumpkin, eggs, and milk, and mix well.

4. Add the dry ingredients to the pumpkin mixture and stir thoroughly. Fold in the nuts and pour into the loaf pan.

5. Bake about 1 hour, or until a cake tester or skewer inserted into the center of the bread comes out clean. Remove from the pan and cool on a rack. This bread freezes well.

Desserts

*I*f Thanksgiving isn't all about desserts, you can't prove it by our family. During the month leading up to the holiday, they freely offer advice about what desserts they think should appear on the dining room sideboard on the big day. Of course, each child has a personal wish list, so we end up making a selection—six or more desserts to satisfy all yearnings.

We feel that Thanksgiving desserts should reflect the bounty of the harvest season. Pumpkins, pears, persimmons, apples, chestnuts, and cranberries are appropriate seasonal ingredients that give a singular flavor to the holiday table. Certain other fruits—bananas, coconut, strawberries among them—just don't seem to fit in. They are representatives of other seasons, other places, and other celebrations.

The desserts that follow have all stood the test of time and diverse palates. These are the sweets that we are proud to serve at our own holiday feast. Most of them are our family favorites, and some are traditions at the tables of friends.

Basic Pumpkin Purée

A number of recipes in the book call for pumpkin purée. Although the canned versions are quite acceptable, there is nothing like doing it all from scratch. A 4-pound pumpkin will yield about 4 cups purée.

Method 1

One 4-pound pumpkin

1. Preheat the oven to 400 degrees. Peel, seed, and cut the pumpkin into 2-inch chunks. Place the pumpkin in a 5-quart ovenproof casserole. Add ¼ inch water. Cover and bake in the oven until tender, about 20 minutes.

2. Pour off any moisture that remains. Purée the pumpkin in a food processor fitted with the metal blade.

Method 2

One 4-pound pumpkin

1. Preheat the oven to 350 degrees. Split and seed the pumpkin, place the 2 halves cut side down in a roasting pan containing 1 cup of water. Bake in the oven until tender, about 90 minutes.

2. Scoop the pulp out of each half and purée in a food processor fitted with the metal blade.

Method 3

One 4-pound pumpkin   5 tablespoons unsalted butter

1. Preheat the oven to 400 degrees. Peel, seed, and cut a 4-pound pumpkin into 2-inch chunks. Melt the butter in a Pyrex baking pan, large enough to fit the pumpkin pieces in one layer, by placing it in the oven for 2 minutes. Put the pumpkin pieces into the baking pan and coat them with the butter. Bake in the oven for 15 minutes. Turn the pieces over and baste. Continue to bake until tender, about 15 more minutes.

2. Purée in a food processor fitted with the metal blade.

Pie Crust

*T*his dough can't miss; it makes a great, flaky crust.

Makes 1 9-inch crust

1 cup all-purpose flour	1 tablespoon beaten egg
Pinch of salt	1 teaspoon vinegar
½ cup vegetable shortening	2 tablespoons water

1. Mix the flour, salt, and shortening in a bowl until crumbly in texture.

2. In another bowl, beat the egg, vinegar, and water until fluffy. Pour this mixture into the bowl with the flour mixture. Mix and knead to combine, but don't overwork the dough. Chill overnight.

NOTE: We generally make this dough in large quantities, usually a triple recipe. The dough keeps well in the freezer. Here are the measurements we use. This makes three 9-inch open-face pies:

3 cups all-purpose flour	1 beaten egg
1 teaspoon salt	1 tablespoon vinegar
1½ cups shortening	6 tablespoons water

Our Favorite Pumpkin Pie

No Thanksgiving is complete without pumpkin pie, but all pumpkin pies are not created equal. There are, of course, various things that can be done with seasonings, crusts, and other ingredients to make a pie unique and memorable. What we have done here is provide our pumpkin pie recipe along with a number of variations. Our favorite invention is among them.

Yes, pumpkin pie can be made without the cream but, to us, it's not as good.

Serves 8 to 12

Pie Crust (see page 150)	1 teaspoon vanilla extract
2 cups pumpkin purée, fresh (see page 148) or canned	1 tablespoon brandy (optional)
	½ teaspoon ground allspice
2 eggs	½ teaspoon freshly grated
1½ cups heavy cream	nutmeg
¾ cup maple syrup	½ teaspoon powdered ginger

1. Preheat the oven to 350 degrees. Line a 9-inch pie pan with the pastry, leaving a ½-inch overlap around the top. Fold the upper edge of the crust back, doubling the amount of crust at the rim of the plate. You can decorate the rim by fluting the edge: With your right index finger gently press forward while at the same time press with the other index finger in the opposite direction. You can also use the tines of a serving fork to make a pattern.

2. In a large bowl combine pumpkin, eggs, cream, and maple syrup. Stir in vanilla and the brandy, if you are using it.

3. In a small bowl, combine spices and mix together. Sprinkle over the pumpkin mixture and blend completely.

4. Pour into the prepared pie shell and bake for 1 hour. The pie is done when a knife tip inserted into the center comes away clean. (To avoid the unsightly mark of this test you can also shake the pie slightly. If the center is firm, the pie is done.) Cool on a wire rack.

VARIATIONS: This pie can be completely changed by varying the seasonings. In all of these variations eliminate the brandy, allspice, nutmeg, and powdered ginger and add the following:

1. This is our favorite because it really amplifies the true flavor of pumpkin. Replace the spices with 1 teaspoon freshly ground white pepper.

(continued)

2. Use 1 tablespoon freshly grated nutmeg and 2 teaspoons finely chopped crystallized ginger.

3. Use 1 tablespoon freshly grated nutmeg, 1 tablespoon finely chopped crystallized ginger, and, instead of maple syrup, ¾ cup brown sugar.

4. Use 1 tablespoon freshly grated nutmeg, ½ cup apricot preserves, and, instead of maple syrup, ½ cup brown sugar.

ADVANCE PREPARATION: Can be made 1 day ahead. Cover and refrigerate. Bring to room temperature before serving.

Pumpkin-Ginger Cheesecake

*H*ere is an interesting Thanksgiving idea that became a great dessert. We tried this on a dare and it has become a mainstay of the holiday table.

Serves 10 to 12

CRUST

1½ cups graham cracker crumbs	1 tablespoon sugar
1 teaspoon ground cinnamon	8 tablespoons (1 stick) unsalted
1 teaspoon ground ginger	butter, melted

FILLING

Three 8-ounce packages cream cheese, at room temperature	1 tablespoon vanilla extract
1½ cups sugar	2 tablespoons dark rum
5 eggs	2 tablespoons minced crystallized ginger
One 16-ounce can pumpkin purée, or 2 cups fresh purée (see page 146)	2 teaspoons ground cinnamon
	½ teaspoon freshly grated nutmeg

TOPPING

1½ cups sour cream	½ teaspoon ground cinnamon
½ cup sugar	2 tablespoons dark rum

1. In the bowl of a food processor fitted with the metal blade, combine graham cracker crumbs, cinnamon, ginger, sugar, and the melted butter, pulsing 2 or 3 times to blend evenly. Pour into a buttered 10-inch spring-form pan and press the mixture onto the bottom and one-third up the sides of the pan. Chill for 30 minutes.

2. Preheat the oven to 325 degrees. In the bowl of an electric mixer beat the cheese and sugar with the paddle beater until smooth. Continuing to beat at medium speed, add the eggs one by one, beating well after each addition.

3. In a mixing bowl combine the pumpkin with the vanilla, rum, ginger, cinnamon, and nutmeg. Mix until smooth. Add the pumpkin mixture to the cream cheese in the mixer, and beat to combine.

4. Pour the filling into the crust and bake for 1½ hours, or until set.

5. Whisk the sour cream, sugar, cinnamon, and rum together and spread over the cake. Allow to cool and then chill for at least 5 hours before serving.

ADVANCE PREPARATION: Can be made up to 2 days ahead. Cover and refrigerate.

Pumpkin Praline Pie

$\mathcal{D}$iane Rossen Worthington is one of America's best cookbook authors, and her Pumpkin Praline Pie is a knockout. Diane suggests using a tart pan for an elegant presentation.

Makes 1 9-inch pie or 1 11-inch tart

PASTRY

1½ cups cake flour
Pinch of salt
1 tablespoon coarsely chopped
  pecans

1 tablespoon confectioners' sugar
9 tablespoons unsalted butter,
  frozen, cut into small pieces
¼ cup cold water

FILLING

3 eggs
⅔ cup granulated sugar
2 cups pumpkin purée, fresh (see
  page 146) or canned
½ teaspoon freshly grated nutmeg

½ teaspoon ground ginger
½ teaspoon ground allspice
Salt
¼ cup half-and-half
3 tablespoons bourbon

TOPPING

¾ cup light brown sugar
4 tablespoons unsalted butter,
  melted

2 tablespoons heavy cream
⅔ cup coarsely chopped pecans
½ cup pecan halves

GARNISH

½ cup heavy cream

1 teaspoon vanilla extract

   1. Preheat the oven to 400 degrees.

   2. For the pastry: Combine flour, salt, pecans, and confectioners' sugar in a food processor fitted with the steel blade. Process a few seconds to blend. Add butter and process until the mixture resembles coarse meal, about 5 to 10 seconds.

   3. With the blade of the processor turning, gradually add water until dough is just beginning to come together. It should adhere when pinched.

4. Transfer the dough to a floured pastry board or work surface. Press into a round shape for easy rolling. Roll out the dough large enough to fit an 11-inch flan ring placed on a baking sheet, an 11-inch tart pan with a removable bottom, or a 9-inch pie shell. Drape the dough circle over a rolling pin and fit into the pan. Press into the pan and cut off excess dough with a knife.

5. Place the tart pan or pie plate on a baking sheet. Press the pastry with fingers so that it adheres to the sides of pan. If using a tart pan with straight edges, raise edges of pastry ¼ to ½ inch above top of pan. With your right index finger gently press forward, while at the same time a little to the left, press your left index finger in the opposing direction to make a fluting edge.

6. Cover crust with a sheet of parchment paper or foil and press to fit sides. Pour baking beads, beans, or rice into center of paper and distribute evenly.

7. Bake crust for 8 minutes. Remove from the oven and lift out the paper and beans. Prick the pastry and return it to the oven for 5 minutes. Remove from the oven and let cool 15 minutes.

8. For the filling: Using electric mixer or a food processor fitted with the steel blade, beat eggs and sugar until light, thick, and lemon-colored, about 3 minutes. Add remaining filling ingredients and mix well. Pour into the cooled pie shell.

9. Bake 15 minutes, then reduce oven temperature to 350 degrees. Bake an additional 35 to 40 minutes, or until set. Remove from the oven and let it cool to room temperature.

10. For the topping: Combine sugar, butter, cream, and chopped pecans, and mix well. Spread evenly over the pie. Garnish with pecan halves.

11. Preheat the broiler. Place the pie under the broiler, turning until topping browns evenly. Make sure it doesn't burn. Leaving the door ajar during this procedure is a good idea.

12. For the garnish: Whip the cream with vanilla in a chilled bowl until fairly stiff. Serve the pie warm; pass whipped cream separately.

ADVANCE PREPARATION: This may be prepared up to 8 hours ahead through step 10 and kept in the refrigerator. Bring to room temperature before continuing. Heat before serving.

Perfect Pecan Pie

*P*ecan pie is almost as essential to Thanksgiving as pumpkin pie. The problem we have found with many recipes is that they have an unappealing, gloppy cornstarch filling. We set about developing a pecan pie that is mainly pecans—no filler. The result is a pecan lover's dream: great to look at and packed with nuts.

Serves 8 to 12

Pie Crust (see page 150), ½ recipe for Flaky Pie Crust (see page 151), or the pecan crust from recipe for Pumpkin Praline Pie (see page 156)

4 tablespoons unsalted butter, softened

¾ cup firmly packed dark brown sugar

3 eggs, at room temperature

1 teaspoon maple syrup

1 teaspoon vanilla extract

1½ tablespoons freshly squeezed orange juice

¾ cup dark corn syrup

2½ cups coarsely chopped pecans

1½ cups unbroken pecan halves

1. Preheat the oven to 425 degrees. Roll the pastry into a round on a lightly floured surface. Line a 9-inch pie pan with the pastry, leaving a ½-inch overlap around the top. Fold the upper edge of the crust back, doubling the amount of crust at the rim of the plate. You can decorate the rim by fluting the edge: With your right index finger gently press forward, while at the same time pressing with the left index finger in the opposite direction. You can also use the tines of a serving fork to make a pattern.

2. Cover pan with a sheet of parchment paper or foil and press to fit sides. Pour baking beads, beans, or rice into center of paper and distribute evenly.

3. Bake crust for 10 minutes. Remove from the oven and lift out the paper and beans. Prick the pastry and let it cool 15 minutes.

4. In the bowl of a mixer, cream the butter and sugar until quite light in color, about 7 minutes. Add the eggs, one at a time, beating 2 minutes after each addition.

5. In a small bowl, combine maple syrup, vanilla, and orange juice.

6. With the mixer at medium speed, alternate adding the corn syrup and the vanilla mixture. Fold in the chopped nuts. Pour into the prebaked pie shell.

7. Place the whole pecans in neat concentric circles on top of the filling.

8. Reduce oven temperature to 350 degrees, and bake the pie in the center of the oven until the filling is set, about 50 minutes. If the pecans on top brown too quickly, cover them with foil until the last 5 minutes of baking time.

ADVANCE PREPARATION: The pie shell can be prepared 1 day ahead through step 3. Once finished, the pie will keep in the refrigerator for 2 days.

Chocolate Pecan Pie

$\mathcal{T}$his delectable variation on the traditional pecan pie was suggested to us by Amanda Lyon.

Serves 8 to 12

Pie Crust (see page 150), ½ recipe for Flaky Pie Crust (see page 151), or the pecan crust from recipe for Pumpkin Praline Pie (see page 156)	¼ cup molasses
	¾ cup light corn syrup
	⅓ cup unsalted butter, melted
	1 tablespoon vanilla extract
3 eggs	¾ cup grated semi-sweet chocolate
1 cup sugar	1½ cups pecan halves

1. Preheat the oven to 425 degrees. Roll the pastry into a round on a lightly floured surface. Line a 9-inch pie pan with the pastry, leaving a ½-inch overlap around the top. Fold the upper edge of the crust back, doubling the amount of crust at the rim of the plate. You can decorate the rim by fluting the edge: With your right index finger gently press forward, while at the same time pressing with the left index finger in the opposite direction. You can also use the tines of a serving fork to make a pattern.

2. Cover pan with a sheet of parchment paper or foil and press to fit sides. Pour baking beads, beans, or rice into center of paper and distribute evenly.

3. Bake crust for 10 minutes. Remove from the oven and lift out the paper and beans. Prick the pastry and let it cool 15 minutes.

(continued)

4. In the bowl of a mixer, beat the eggs with the sugar until the mixture turns a pale yellow and forms a ribbon when dropped from the beater. Add the molasses, corn syrup, melted butter, and vanilla. Mix to combine. Add the grated chocolate and the pecans.

5. Pour the filling into the pie shell. Reduce oven temperature to 350 degrees, and bake the pie in the center of the oven until the filling is set, about 50 minutes. Test for doneness with a cake tester.

ADVANCE PREPARATION: The pie shell can be prepared 1 day ahead through step 3. Once finished, the pie will keep in the refrigerator for 2 days. Bring to room temperature before serving.

Almond Tart

*T*his is a knockout dessert that offers an elegant alternative to pecan pie. It is buttery, rich, and quite superb.

Serves 8 to 12

CRUST

1½ cups all-purpose flour
Pinch of salt
2 tablespoons sugar
8 tablespoons (1 stick) unsalted
   butter, chilled

½ teaspoon almond extract
1 egg, separated
2 to 3 tablespoons ice water

FILLING

¾ cup sugar
8 tablespoons (1 stick) unsalted
   butter
2 tablespoons honey
½ cup heavy cream

1¾ cups sliced blanched almonds
   (about 8 ounces)
1 tablespoon Grand Marnier, or
   other orange liqueur
¼ teaspoon almond extract

Sweetened whipped cream (optional)

1. For the crust: Butter a 9-inch tart pan with a removable bottom (it can be fluted or smooth). In the bowl of a food processor fitted with the metal blade, combine flour, salt, and sugar by pulsing on and off for a few seconds. Cut the butter in small pieces and add all to the flour mixture. Add almond extract and the egg yolk. Pulse again for a few seconds, until the mixture resembles coarse meal. Be careful not to overprocess.

2. With the blades of the processor turning, add the water gradually, until the dough is just beginning to come together and will adhere when pinched.

3. Roll out the dough on a lightly floured surface into a ⅛-inch thick round, about 12 inches in diameter. Place the dough in the tart pan by draping it over the rolling pin and gently unrolling it into place. Fold the excess over to give the sides of the crust a double thickness. Press neatly into the sides of the tart pan. Prick the bottom several times with a fork. Refrigerate at least 30 minutes. (Can be prepared 1 day ahead. Cover and refrigerate.)

4. Preheat the oven to 325 degrees. Line the tart shell with foil or parchment and gently press to fit sides. Place enough baking beads, beans, or rice in the crust to fill it. Bake in the preheated oven for 15 minutes. Remove foil or parchment and weights. Lightly brush crust with beaten egg white. Bake until crust is light golden brown, about 15 more minutes. Cool completely on a rack.

5. For the filling: Preheat the oven to 375 degrees. In a heavy 2-quart saucepan cook sugar, butter, and honey over low heat, stirring until the sugar dissolves. Increase the heat to medium and cook until the sugar is golden brown, stirring frequently, about 3 minutes. Remove from the heat.

6. Stir in the cream (the mixture will bubble). Return to the heat and stir until well blended. Mix in the almonds, Grand Marnier, and almond extract. Remove from heat. Let stand 15 minutes. Gently ladle the almond filling into the crust. Bake in the preheated oven until the filling bubbles vigorously all over, about 20 minutes.

7. Cool the tart in the pan on a rack until set, about 4 hours.

8. Remove the tart from the pan. Cut it into wedges and serve topped with dollops of whipped cream, if desired.

ADVANCE PREPARATION: Can be prepared 1 day ahead. When cool, cover with plastic wrap and let stand at room temperature.

Thanksgiving Dinner

Apple Pie

*T*he secret of a great apple pie is the apples. They must be fresh, crisp, hard, and tart. Look for Granny Smiths, Pippins, or Jonathans, and avoid the soft, bland ones, such as Delicious.

Serves 8 to 12

Flaky Pie Crust (see page 151)
½ cup light brown sugar
2 tablespoons flour
1 teaspoon cinnamon
1 teaspoon freshly grated
　nutmeg

6 to 7 large tart apples, peeled,
　cored, and quartered
Juice of 1 orange
2 tablespoons unsalted butter

1. On a lightly floured surface, roll out the dough into 2 rounds, ⅛-inch thick. Use 1 to line the bottom of a 9-inch pie pan. Roll up the second round between 2 pieces of wax paper and refrigerate along with the pie shell.

2. In a small bowl, combine the brown sugar, flour, cinnamon, and nutmeg.

3. Cut each apple quarter into 4 slices. In a large bowl, toss the apples with the orange juice. Combine the brown sugar mixture with the apples. Toss to coat. Let the apples stand, at room temperature, for 1 hour.

4. Preheat the oven to 450 degrees. Using a slotted spoon, fill the pie shell with the apples. They should rise at least 1 inch above the rim. Discard the liquid that collects in the bottom of the apple bowl. Dot the apples with butter. Moisten the rim of the bottom crust with water and cover with the second round of dough, crimping the top to the bottom with your fingers or a serving fork. Cut 4 symmetrical slits in the top crust.

5. Bake in the preheated oven for 15 minutes. Reduce the heat to 350 degrees and bake for an additional 30 minutes more.

ADVANCE PREPARATION: This pie does not improve with age, but it can be prepared 1 day ahead. Store at room temperature. Reheat in a 250-degree oven.

Cranberry Apple Pie

*T*his excellent variation on the traditional apple pie is the brainchild of Peggi McGlynn, one of San Francisco's best cooks.

Serves 8 to 12

Flaky Pie Crust (see page 151)
3 cups fresh or frozen
    cranberries
4 large tart apples, peeled,
    cored, and quartered
1 cup maple syrup

4 teaspoons cornstarch dissolved
    in 2 tablespoons cold water
1 teaspoon freshly grated
    nutmeg
2 tablespoons unsalted butter

1. On a lightly floured surface, roll out the dough into 2 rounds, ⅛-inch thick. Use 1 to line the bottom of a 9-inch pie pan. Roll up the second round between 2 pieces of wax paper and refrigerate along with the pie shell.

2. In a medium saucepan, combine cranberries, apples, and maple syrup. Over medium heat, bring the mixture to a boil. Reduce the heat to a simmer and cook until the cranberries have popped, about 4 minutes. Stir the cornstarch mixture into the fruit and simmer until thickened, about 1 more minute. Grate in the nutmeg.

3. Preheat the oven to 450 degrees. Using a slotted spoon, fill the pie shell with the cranberry-apple mixture. Dot the fruit with butter. Moisten the rim of the bottom crust with water and cover with the second round of dough, crimping the top to the bottom with your fingers or the tines of a serving fork. Cut 4 symmetrical slits in the top crust.

4. Bake in the preheated oven for 15 minutes. Reduce the heat to 350 degrees and bake for 30 minutes more.

VARIATION: Roll out the top crust and cut it in strips with a fluted pastry knife. Refrigerate the strips on a baking sheet for 10 minutes. Once the shell is filled, weave the lattice strips over the fruit in a decorative design.

ADVANCE PREPARATION: This pie does not improve with age, but it can be prepared 1 day ahead. Store at room temperature. Reheat in a 250-degree oven.

Jessica's Caramelized Apple Tart

$\mathcal{T}$his easy dessert, based on the French *Tarte Tatin,* goes apple pie one step better—it coats the apples in a toasty caramel syrup. Not only is this wonderfully delicious, but it is remarkably easy. For Thanksgiving we generally try to avoid any dishes that require last-minute preparation, but this is so yummy, and so simple to make, that we made an exception.

Serves 8 to 10

½ recipe Flaky Pie Crust (page 151)
6 tablespoons unsalted butter
¾ cup sugar

5 or 6 hard green apples (such as Granny Smiths), peeled and cut into quarters

1. On a well-floured surface, roll out the dough to a round about 10 inches across. Place the dough between 2 sheets of wax paper, roll into a tube shape, and refrigerate. This can be done the day before.

2. Preheat the oven to 400 degrees. In an ovenproof and nonstick 10-inch skillet, melt the butter. Add the sugar and stir until dissolved. Then add the apples to the skillet, round side down, using just enough apple so that the pieces fit snugly in the pan. Sauté over medium heat until the sugar begins to turn golden brown, indicating that it is caramelizing. Do not stir. This process should take about 20 minutes.

3. Place the skillet in the preheated oven for 5 minutes. Carefully remove it from the oven and unroll the chilled dough over the top, tucking the dough inside the rim of the skillet. Increase the oven temperature to 450 degrees. Return the skillet to the oven and bake for 20 minutes or until the crust is brown and crisp.

4. Remove from the oven and quickly reverse onto a cake plate. Scoop any caramel or apple sections that remain in the bottom of the skillet over the tart and serve immediately.

Apricot-Cranberry Dessert

This started as a condiment, but it turned out to be a great dessert with a refreshingly tangy flavor and a bright color.

Makes 6 cups (12 ½-cup servings)

1¼ cups superfine sugar
1⅓ cups water
1 cup cranberries

12 ounces dried apricots
2 navel oranges

1. In a small saucepan combine half the sugar with ⅔ cup water. Stir to dissolve and bring to a boil. Add the cranberries. Simmer gently for 5 minutes, just until the berries start to pop.

2. Remove from the heat and pour into a small bowl. Allow the berries to come to room temperature before chilling. Cover and chill at least 4 hours; for best results, refrigerate overnight.

3. In another small saucepan combine the remaining sugar and ⅔ cup water and dissolve as before. This time, boil the syrup. Add the apricots and toss to coat in the sugar glaze, but do not stir. Let cook, carefully watching to avoid burning. (Apricots are delightful when caramelized to a very light amber color; if cooked too long the fruit becomes tough. To avoid this, have a bowl of cold water large enough to hold the pan. When you reach the light caramel stage, submerge the pan in the water to stop the process.) When done, transfer the apricots to a bowl immediately.

4. Slice the zest off the oranges, removing all of the white pith. Cut out the segments by slicing down into the center of the fruit next to each membrane separation. Leave the segments in the shape of wedges. Julienne the peel and add to the oranges.

5. Combine the cranberries, apricots, and orange segments. Chill for at least 1 hour before serving.

ADVANCE PREPARATION: Can be made 2 or 3 days ahead. Cover and refrigerate. This dessert improves with time.

Pear Mincemeat Pie

*T*his modern mincemeat foregoes the traditional beef suet and as a result it is considerably more digestible and—we think—better tasting than the heavy and very time-consuming old-style mincemeat.

Serves 8 to 12

1 lemon
½ cup firmly packed dark brown
    sugar
1 cup coarsely chopped currants
½ cup coarsely chopped golden
    raisins
1 cup coarsely chopped
    cranberries
2 pounds firm pears, peeled,
    cored, and coarsely chopped
¾ cup apple cider
2 tablespoons unsulfured
    molasses
1 teaspoon vanilla extract

1 teaspoon ground cinnamon
½ teaspoon freshly grated
    nutmeg
¼ teaspoon ground ginger
¼ teaspoon ground allspice
Pinch of freshly ground pepper
1 cup walnuts, toasted and
    coarsely chopped
⅓ cup Calvados or apple brandy
2 tablespoons unsalted butter
Pie Crust (see page 150),
    doubled
1 egg white, beaten

1. Slice the peel from the lemon with a sharp knife or a vegetable peeler. Cut off any of the white pith from the pieces of peel. Mince the peel. After cutting the pith from the lemon, chop the lemon coarsely. Put the minced peel and the lemon into a 2-quart saucepan with the brown sugar.

2. In the bowl of a food processor fitted with the metal blade, place the currants, raisins, cranberries, pears, apple cider, molasses, vanilla, and spices. Pulse 4 to 5 times. Add to the saucepan containing the lemon peel.

3. Place the saucepan over medium heat and bring to a simmer. Reduce the heat and continue to simmer for 30 minutes, stirring occasionally.

4. Preheat the oven to 350 degrees (or use a toaster oven). Toast the walnuts for 20 minutes. Chop coarsely.

5. Add the brandy to the raisin-cranberry mixture and simmer for an additional 5 minutes. Remove from the heat and stir in the walnuts and butter.

6. Line a 9-inch pie plate with a circle of pie crust dough. Pierce the bottom several times with a fork. Fill—but don't overfill—with the mincemeat. Top with the other circle of dough, crimping the edges and piercing the top several times with a small, sharp knife. Brush the top surface with egg white. Bake until the crust is deep golden brown, about 40 minutes. Cool to room temperature before serving.

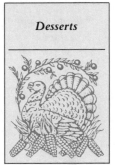

VARIATION: If you don't want to make a pie, this mincemeat is very pleasant as a condiment or as a dessert on its own. Just complete the recipe to the end of step 5. It will make 5 cups of mincemeat.

You can also substitute apples for pears and/or pecans for the walnuts.

ADVANCE PREPARATION: The mincemeat can be made as much as 1 week in advance. The completed pie can be prepared 1 day ahead. Cover and store at room temperature.

Pear Cobbler with Prunes and Armagnac

*H*ere's an easy, all-American dessert from Susan Lifrieri, the pastry chef of the Manhattan Ocean Club in New York City.

Serves 10 to 12

FILLING

1 cup pitted prunes
½ cup Armagnac
8 ripe pears
4 tablespoons unsalted butter

¾ cup granulated sugar
1 tablespoon freshly squeezed
  lemon juice

CRUST

1 cup all-purpose flour
2 tablespoons granulated sugar
¼ teaspoon salt
2 teaspoons baking powder
4 tablespoons unsalted butter
6 tablespoons milk

2 tablespoons unsalted butter,
  melted
2 tablespoons superfine sugar
Crème fraîche or Devonshire
  double cream (optional)

1. For the filling: Marinate the prunes in the Armagnac for 1 or 2 days, or until soft.

(continued)

2. Peel, core, and slice the pears into pieces ¼ inch thick. Heat a skillet over moderate heat and melt 2 tablespoons butter and ¼ cup sugar. Add the pear slices and sauté them until they are glazed with the sugar, about 2 minutes. Add the liquid from the prunes and cook until the liquid is reduced by half. Remove from the heat and cool.

3. Remove the pears from the skillet with a slotted spoon and place them in an 8-inch-square baking dish. Place the skillet over high heat and reduce the liquid in the pan until it becomes a thick syrup.

4. Add the prunes to the pears and stir to distribute evenly. Pour the pan syrup and the lemon juice over the fruit. Sprinkle with the remaining ½ cup sugar. Dot the top with the remaining 2 tablespoons of butter. Set aside.

5. For the crust: Preheat the oven to 425 degrees. Combine all the dry ingredients. Cut in the butter and mix until the dough has an even, crumbly consistency.

6. Add the milk and mix until combined. The dough should be sticky and soft. Place it on a well-floured surface and knead until it holds a shape. (Use no more than ten turns or the dough will be tough.)

7. Roll out the dough about ½ inch thick, until it is large enough to cover the fruit in the baking dish. Trim the edges and tuck the dough around the fruit. Brush the melted butter over the dough and sprinkle with the superfine sugar.

8. Bake in the preheated oven for 40 minutes, or until the crust is golden and the fruit is tender when pierced.

9. Remove from the oven and cool slightly before serving. Serve right from the baking dish. Garnish with crème fraîche or Devonshire double cream.

ADVANCE PREPARATION: Can be prepared 1 day ahead. Cover and refrigerate. Bring to room temperature before baking.

Nana's Walnut Torte

*T*his cake, handed down by Mary Powell's great-grandmother, is an old-fashioned masterpiece. It is big and dramatic and incredibly delicious. This is the cake you would imagine your grandmother making—if your grandmother was a good cook.

Serves 16

THE CAKE

2 cups walnuts
9 eggs
2 cups sugar
Juice of 1 lemon
½ teaspoon salt

¼ teaspoon ground cloves
¾ cup cake flour
2 teaspoons baking powder
Grated zest of 2 lemons

MOCHA FROSTING

½ pound (2 sticks) unsalted
   butter, at room temperature
3 cups confectioners' sugar
1 tablespoon instant espresso
   crystals
1 tablespoon hot water

2 tablespoons all-purpose ground
   chocolate or cocoa
1 teaspoon vanilla extract
½ cup heavy cream
1 cup chopped walnuts

1. For the cake: Preheat the oven to 350 degrees. Butter three 9-inch cake pans and dust with flour.

2. Using a hand nut grinder, finely grind the walnuts. (Do not use the processor for this, it will overprocess the nuts and make them oily. They should be fluffy and dry.)

3. Separate 8 of the eggs. Place the yolks and the 1 remaining whole egg in a mixer bowl. Add 1 cup sugar, the lemon juice, salt, and ground cloves. Combine well in the mixer bowl and, while beating at slow speed, add the remaining sugar. Raise speed to high and beat until the yolk mixture is light and fluffy and almost doubled in bulk, about 7 minutes. Transfer to a large bowl.

4. Sift the cake flour and baking powder together into another bowl.

5. Beat the 8 egg whites in a clean mixer bowl until they are stiff but not dry. Fold one-third of the egg yolk mixture into the egg whites, then add one-third of the flour mixture, nuts, and lemon zest. Repeat until all elements are combined.

(continued)

6. Divide the batter among the three prepared pans. Reduce the oven temperature to 325 degrees and bake for 40 minutes, or until done. Cool on a wire rack.

7. For the frosting: Whip the butter and add the sugar in small amounts. Continue whipping until the mixture is very light and fluffy. Dissolve the instant coffee in the hot water and add, with the chocolate and vanilla, to the butter and sugar mixture. Beat until fluffy.

8. Beat the cream until stiff. Fold in half of the mocha mixture.

9. Smooth the mocha-cream mixture between the three layers of cake. Use the remaining mocha frosting on the top and sides of the cake. Decorate the sides with chopped walnuts.

NOTE: For the mocha frosting, we use Ghirardelli ground chocolate. If you can't find this product, substitute cocoa.

ADVANCE PREPARATION: Can be prepared 1 day ahead. Cover and refrigerate.

Amanda's Chocolate Carrot Torte

A dazzling version of the traditional carrot cake, this is a staple in our kitchen where its life expectancy is about a day or maybe two, at the most. For the holidays, dress it up with a sprinkling of confectioners' sugar and serve it with the Apricot-Cranberry Dessert on page 165.

Serves 8 to 12

¾ cup stale white bread crumbs
2 cups blanched whole almonds
1½ cups sugar
7 ounces bittersweet chocolate, broken in pieces
5 medium carrots, peeled and grated

6 eggs
½ teaspoon almond extract
1 teaspoon vanilla extract
1 teaspoon instant espresso crystals

1. Preheat oven to 350 degrees. Butter a 9-inch bundt pan and refrigerate.

2. In a food processor fitted with the metal blade, place the bread crumbs, almonds, and ½ cup of the sugar. Process for 30 seconds. The mixture should be ground into a coarse meal. Pour into a 3-quart bowl.

3. After wiping out the processor bowl, process the chocolate chunks with ½ cup of sugar until that mixture is the same consistency as the almonds. Combine the chocolate with the almond mixture. Wipe out the food processor again and fit it with a fine grating blade.

4. Cut the carrots in 2-inch lengths. Fit them into the large feed tube and grate. Add the carrots to the chocolate-almond mixture, tossing to mix. Create a well in the center of this mixture.

5. In the bowl of an electric mixer, whip the eggs at medium speed for 3 minutes. Add the final ½ cup of sugar. Turn the mixer to the highest speed, and run for 7 minutes. The eggs should be at a ribbon stage. To test this, remove the beater and hold it over the mixture; it should form a ribbon as it drips from the beater. Add almond and vanilla extracts and coffee crystals.

6. Turn this batter into the center of the well in the chocolate-almond mixture. Using a rubber spatula, fold the egg mixture into the chocolate-almond combination. Continue folding until completely incorporated.

7. Pour into the prepared pan and bake for 1 hour. Test before removing from the oven. This cake makes a crusty surface so you have to press harder than normal to have the cake spring back.

8. When done, allow to cool on a rack for 15 minutes. Then gently unmold and finish cooling on a wire rack.

ADVANCE PREPARATION: Can be prepared 2 days in advance. Cover and store at room temperature.

Ginger-Applesauce Spice Cake
with Ginger Whipped Cream

*T*his delicious moist cake is always popular because it has a texture and flavor that contrasts nicely with some of the dense and rich Thanksgiving desserts.

Serves 8 to 12

2 cups all-purpose flour
1½ teaspoons baking soda
1 teaspoon ground allspice
1 teaspoon ground cinnamon
½ teaspoon ground cloves
½ teaspoon salt
12 tablespoons (1½ sticks) unsalted butter, softened
1 cup firmly packed dark brown sugar
½ cup superfine sugar
2 large eggs, at room temperature

1⅓ cups unsweetened applesauce
⅔ cup sour cream
¾ cup lightly toasted, coarsely chopped walnuts (about 3 ounces)
⅓ cup peeled, minced fresh gingerroot

Confectioners' sugar
Ginger Whipped Cream (see below)

1. Position rack in the center of the oven and preheat the oven to 350 degrees.

2. Butter a 9 x 3-inch springform pan. Dust lightly with flour; tap out the excess.

3. Sift the flour, baking soda, allspice, cinnamon, cloves, and salt into a medium bowl. Using an electric mixer, beat the butter with both sugars in a large bowl until well combined. Add the eggs, one at a time, beating well after each addition.

4. Beat in the applesauce and sour cream (the mixture may appear curdled). Add the dry ingredients, walnuts, and ginger and mix until just combined.

5. Pour the batter into the prepared pan. Place the pan on a cookie sheet in the center of the preheated oven. Bake for 1 hour, or until a toothpick or cake tester inserted into the center of the cake comes out clean.

6. Let the cake cool in its pan on a rack for 15 minutes. Run a small sharp knife around the cake sides to loosen it. Release the pan sides from

the cake. Remove the springform and let the cake cool another 15 minutes or so.

7. When cool, dust the top of the cake with confectioners' sugar, or place a paper doilie on top of the cake and dusk with confectioners' sugar, then remove the doilie and you will have a pretty, lacy design.

8. Serve with a dollop of Ginger Whipped Cream on each piece.

Ginger Whipped Cream

½ cup sugar	1 cup chilled heavy cream
½ cup water	1 tablespoon confectioners'
One 1½-inch piece fresh	sugar
gingerroot, sliced	¼ teaspoon vanilla extract

1. Stir the sugar and water in a heavy medium saucepan over medium heat until the sugar dissolves. Add the ginger and simmer until syrupy, about 8 minutes. Strain into a bowl. Refrigerate the syrup until cold.

2. Using the electric mixer, whip the cream, sugar, and vanilla in a large bowl to soft peaks. Fold in the syrup.

ADVANCE PREPARATION: The cake can be prepared 6 hours in advance. Cool it completely. Cover tightly and let stand at room temperature. The syrup for the whipped cream can be prepared 3 days ahead. After whipping, the finished cream will hold for 5 hours. Cover and refrigerate. If necessary, whisk before using, to stiffen.

Mama Hellman's Date Cake

*T*his is a dark, airy cake that has great chewy texture and plenty of spicy flavor. It is easy to make and keeps well. The recipe comes from Mary Powell's great-great-grandmother.

Makes 1 9-inch cake

1 cup plus 1 tablespoon sugar
5 eggs, separated
½ teaspoon ground cinnamon
½ teaspoon ground allspice
¼ teaspoon ground cloves
2 tablespoons ground chocolate
   or cocoa

⅔ cup finely chopped dates
½ cup plus 1 teaspoon cracker
   meal or matzo meal
Salt
Confectioners' sugar

1. Preheat the oven to 350 degrees. Butter a 9-inch springform pan, then cut a circle of wax paper to fit its bottom. Butter the wax paper, then flour bottom and sides of pan.

2. With an electric mixer fitted with a paddle beater, slowly cream the sugar and the 5 egg yolks. Add the spices, chocolate, and dates. Blend in the cracker meal or matzo meal.

3. In another bowl whip the egg whites and a pinch of salt until stiff. Fold into the date mixture. Pour the batter into the prepared pan.

4. Bake in the preheated oven for 30 minutes. Lower the heat to 325 degrees and bake 50 minutes more, or until done. The center should be moist.

5. Cool on a rack for 1 hour. Unmold and dust the top with confectioners' sugar.

NOTE: We use Ghirardelli for the ground chocolate. If you can't find this product, substitute cocoa.

VARIATION: Spread each serving plate with a bittersweet chocolate sauce. Place a slice of date cake on top. Then top the cake with whipped cream or Ginger Whipped Cream (page 173).

ADVANCE PREPARATION: Can be prepared 2 days ahead. Cover or wrap with plastic and store at room temperature.

A Different Fruitcake

Fruitcake is controversial in our house. Andy likes it; Kathy doesn't. We made a number of versions, but we couldn't agree on one, until we tried this recipe by Nancy Oakes of L'Avenue Restaurant in San Francisco.

Serves 10 to 12

3 cups homemade unsweetened applesauce
½ pound (2 sticks) unsalted butter
1½ cups sugar
⅓ cup honey
1 cup medium sherry
4 eggs, separated
4 cups slivered almonds
1 cup dried tart cherries (not the candied or glacéed variety)
1 cup chopped dried apricots

1 cup chopped good-quality citron
1 cup chopped good-quality candied pineapple
1 cup white raisins
1 cup currants
5 cups all-purpose flour
1 tablespoon plus 1 teaspoon baking soda
1 teaspoon salt
½ cup brandy

1. Heat the applesauce in a 2-quart saucepan. Add butter a few pieces at a time and stir until it is melted and the applesauce is bubbling. Add sugar, honey, and sherry. Cook until the sugar dissolves. Cool to room temperature. Add 4 egg yolks and mix well.

2. Preheat the oven to 275 degrees. Butter and flour 10 small loaf pans, 5 by 3 by 2 inches, or use one 3-quart decorative tube pan.

3. In a large bowl combine all fruits and nuts with the applesauce. Sift the flour, baking soda, and salt, then fold them into the applesauce mixture. Beat the egg whites to stiff peaks. Fold them into the mixture.

4. Pour into the prepared pans. Smooth the tops and bake for 60 to 70 minutes for small pans, or 2½ to 3 hours for the larger pan.

5. Remove cake(s) from the pans and brush all sides with brandy while the cake is still warm. Let cool. Wrap tightly in plastic wrap and then foil.

ADVANCE PREPARATION: Must be prepared well in advance, at least 1 week, or up to 3 months. If preparing this cake one to three months in advance, brush with brandy once a month.

Moosehead Gingerbread

*I*f there's a way to improve on this traditional New England cake we haven't found it. This is the gingerbread we all dreamed of as children and have only rarely tasted. It is moist, spicy, and loaded with flavor. Great on its own, this is also a fine base for the Gingerbread Bread Pudding on page 180.

Serves 9 to 12

9 tablespoons butter
¼ cup dry bread crumbs
¼ cup chopped crystallized ginger
¼ cup Cognac or brandy
2½ cups all-purpose flour
2 teaspoons baking soda
½ teaspoon salt
1 teaspoon ground cinnamon
1½ teaspoons ground ginger

¼ teaspoon ground cloves
½ teaspoon dry mustard
½ teaspoon freshly ground pepper
½ cup dark brown sugar
2 eggs
1 cup unsulfured molasses
1 tablespoon instant espresso crystals
1 cup boiling water

1. Preheat the oven to 350 degrees. Grease a 9-inch square pan with 1 tablespoon of butter. Dust with the bread crumbs and tap out any excess.

2. In a small bowl, soak the crystallized ginger in the Cognac. Sift the flour, baking soda, salt, cinnamon, ginger, cloves, mustard, and pepper together into another bowl.

3. In the bowl of an electric mixer, cream the remaining butter until it is light and fluffy. Slowly add the brown sugar. Whip until fluffy. Add the eggs, one at a time, while continuing to beat. Add the molasses.

4. Dissolve the espresso in the boiling water. Add the hot liquid to the butter mixture, ¼ cup at a time, alternating with the flour mixture, until both are fully incorporated. Strain off and discard the liquid from the ginger. Fold the ginger into the batter.

5. Pour the batter into the prepared pan. Smooth the top evenly and bake for 35 minutes, or until a cake tester or skewer inserted in the center of the cake comes out clean. Cool in the pan on a rack for 15 minutes. Invert onto a plate.

ADVANCE PREPARATION: Can be prepared 3 days in advance. Wrap tightly with plastic wrap and refrigerate. If you make the gingerbread 1 day ahead, refrigeration isn't necessary.

Pumpkin Flan

*T*his is a cool and refreshing dessert that is also richly flavored. It is a fine alternative to pumpkin pie if you want to have a dessert that contrasts with the other pies on your holiday table.

Serves 10 to 12

1¼ cups sugar
½ teaspoon salt
½ teaspoon nutmeg
½ teaspoon ground cinnamon
1 cup cooked and mashed
   pumpkin

5 large eggs, lightly beaten
1½ cups evaporated milk
1½ teaspoons vanilla extract
⅓ cup water

1. In a small saucepan, melt ½ cup sugar over medium-low heat until it caramelizes into an amber syrup. Stir continuously to prevent burning. Pour into a 9-inch pie plate. Pick the plate up and tip it from side to side to coat its bottom with caramel.

2. Preheat the oven to 350 degrees. In a bowl, combine the remaining sugar, salt, spices, pumpkin, and eggs. Mix thoroughly and add the milk, vanilla, and water. Mix again and pour into the pie plate. Set in a pan of hot water that comes 1 inch up the sides of the pie plate, and bake for 1¼ hours.

3. Cool on a rack and then refrigerate. To serve, run a thin knife around the outside of the flan. Jiggle the plate gently to loosen the flan, then invert a platter over the pie plate, and, holding the two plates firmly together, quickly flip them over. Center the flan and serve.

ADVANCE PREPARATION: Can be prepared 1 day ahead. Keep the flan in the pie plate, refrigerated, and remove it only when ready to serve.

Persimmon Pudding

*Y*ear after year this wonderful steamed pudding is the favorite dessert at our house on Thanksgiving. Even the kids come back for seconds. The recipe is fairly straightforward and easy to do—the only problem is getting persimmons that are ripe enough. They begin to appear in the market just around Thanksgiving. Unfortunately, they are often unripe—too firm and tannic. A ripe persimmon should be pillow soft and delicately silky inside.

You can ripen persimmons yourself at home by putting them stem side up in a plastic container. Put a few drops of brandy on their stems and close the container tightly. In 3 or 4 days your persimmons should be ripe. Placing them in a tightly sealed brown paper bag accompanied by a banana works almost as well. As a last resort, you can freeze the unripe persimmons. This will not ripen them but, once defrosted, their texture will be softer.

The following recipe, which came from our friend Paige Healy, is for two 2-quart pudding molds (or four 1-quart molds, or any other combination). We like to make two puddings, one for the Thanksgiving table and another that can either be used as a gift or frozen for Christmas. If you want to make only one mold, halve the recipe—it works fine.

Serves 8 to 12

8 to 10 ripe persimmons	5 tablespoons brandy
1¼ cups (2½ sticks) unsalted butter, melted	2½ teaspoons vanilla extract
2½ cups sugar	1 cup raisins
2½ cups all-purpose flour, sifted	1 cup currants, soaked in hot water for 30 minutes
¾ teaspoon salt	2½ teaspoons freshly squeezed lemon juice
2½ teaspoons ground cinnamon	¾ cup coarsely chopped walnuts
3 teaspoons baking soda dissolved in 5 tablespoons hot water	5 eggs, lightly beaten

1. Spoon the pulp out of the persimmons and purée in a food processor or blender. This should make 4 cups of purée. Reserve.

2. In an electric mixer or a large mixing bowl combine the butter and sugar. Stir in the rest of the ingredients, including the persimmon purée, and combine well.

3. Butter the inside of two 2-quart pudding molds. Fill with the per-

simmon mixture and cover tightly. (Most molds have covers that snap on. If you don't have such a mold, use a ring mold and cover tightly with foil.)

4. Preheat the oven to 350 degrees.

5. In a large kettle or stockpot that contains ¾ inch of water, place each mold on a rack or an inverted Pyrex dish. Don't let the water touch the mold. Over medium heat, bring the water to a boil. Reduce the heat to low and cover the pot tightly.

6. Put the kettle in the preheated oven and steam the puddings for 2½ hours, checking frequently to make sure that the water hasn't boiled away. (If it has, add more by dribbling it down the sides of the pot.)

6. When done, let the puddings rest for 5 minutes. Then remove them from the molds and place on a rack to cool.

NOTES: The puddings can be served warm or at room temperature. A festive touch is to flame the pudding and bring it to the table—after having dimmed the lights. Flaming is dangerous and should be done only by someone who has mastered the technique. Take ¼ cup of brandy (or other spirit) and warm over medium heat in a small saucepan. After about 30 seconds, tip the saucepan away from you and, averting your eyes, light by bringing a match close to the warm liquid, but not too close. Pour the flaming spirit over the pudding and serve immediately with Hard Sauce (page 180) or Foamy Brandy Sauce (see page 185).

If you are freezing your pudding, leave it in the mold so that it may be steamed again (about 30 minutes after defrosting).

VARIATION: If necessary, you may steam the puddings on top of the stove over low heat for 2½ hours. But steaming them in the oven ensures more even heating.

ADVANCE PREPARATION: The pudding can be made 3 days before Thanksgiving and kept unrefrigerated in the mold. When ready to serve, steam for 15 minutes. Unmold onto a platter.

Hard Sauce

$\mathcal{A}$ must for steamed puddings.

Makes 1½ cups

8 tablespoons (1 stick) unsalted
  butter

1 cup confectioners' sugar, sifted
3 tablespoons dark rum

In a bowl, cream the butter until soft. Add the sugar ¼ cup at a time, beating it into the butter after each addition. Beat in the rum. Refrigerate to harden. It is helpful to refrigerate the hard sauce in the bowl in which it is to be served.

ADVANCE PREPARATION: Can be prepared up to 3 days in advance. Cover and refrigerate.

Gingerbread Bread Pudding

$\mathcal{M}$eredith Frederick is the talented pastry chef of The Post House, a New York steakhouse. This dish, a regular offering on one of the best dessert carts you've ever seen, is a sensation at the Thanksgiving table.

Serves 9 to 12

1 cup heavy cream
1 quart half-and-half
1 cup golden raisins
5 egg yolks
5 whole eggs

2 cups sugar
¼ cup whiskey
1 tablespoon vanilla extract
1 loaf Moosehead Gingerbread
  (page 176)

1. Preheat the oven to 375 degrees.
2. In a large saucepan, combine the creams and raisins and bring to a boil. Remove from the heat.
3. In a large bowl, combine yolks, whole eggs, sugar, whiskey, and vanilla. Slowly whisk in the cream mixture. Set aside.

4. Layer the bottom of a 9-inch square glass baking dish with thin slices of gingerbread. Ladle enough custard over the gingerbread to cover it. Let it sit for 10 minutes. Continue to layer with custard and gingerbread, allowing 10 minutes resting time in between each layer, until the pan is filled to the brim. Let sit for an additional 10 to 15 minutes.

5. Place the pan inside a larger pan that contains ½ inch of hot water. Bake in the preheated oven for about 40 minutes or until the center tests done by being totally set but not dry.

6. Serve in squares that are warm or at room temperature, accompanied by Whiskey Crème Anglaise.

Whiskey Crème Anglaise

Makes 3 cups

2 cups heavy cream	6 egg yolks
½ cup sugar	¼ cup whiskey

1. Over medium-low heat, scald the cream and ¼ cup of the sugar in a saucepan, whisking constantly.

2. In another saucepan, combine the egg yolks and the remaining sugar. Add the whiskey. Slowly pour the hot cream over the yolk mixture, beating constantly.

3. Stir over medium heat until the sauce thickens just enough to coat the back of a wooden spoon. Remove from the heat immediately and strain through a fine sieve.

4. Chill and serve. (If you want to cool the sauce quickly, place the pan in a larger bowl with crushed ice and stir for a minute or two.)

ADVANCE PREPARATION: The pudding can be prepared 1 day ahead through step 3. Cover and refrigerate the cream mixture. Bring to room temperature before assembling and heating. The whiskey sauce can be made 5 or 6 hours ahead of time.

Philadelphia Vanilla Ice Cream

*T*his eggless ice cream is enormously refreshing. It is similar in texture to the best Italian gelato.

Makes 3 pints (12 ½-cup servings)

5 cups half-and-half
1½ cups sugar
⅛ teaspoon salt

4 vanilla beans (3 inches in length), split lengthwise

1. In the top of a double boiler, combine 3 cups half-and-half, sugar, salt, and vanilla beans. Cook, stirring constantly, for 10 minutes. Remove bean pods, scrape out the pulp, and add back to the half-and-half. Stir well to disperse the tiny seeds, then remove from the heat. Pour into a bowl to cool. Chill overnight.
2. The next day, add the remaining 2 cups of well-chilled half-and-half. Mix well.
3. Freeze in an ice-cream maker, following the manufacturer's instructions.

SERVING SUGGESTION: Top with fruit, syrup, or mix with any number of flavors or ingredients such as chopped chocolate, malt, praline, chopped nuts, or candied fruits.

ADVANCE PREPARATION: Although this ice cream is best when served immediately, it will keep 2 weeks in the freezer. When ready to use, soften at room temperature.

Caramel Ice Cream

*T*his luscious ice cream is a Wolfgang Puck specialty. It is delectable on its own and as an accompaniment to pumpkin or apple pie.

Makes 3 pints (12 ½-cup servings)

1⅔ cups sugar	1 cup milk
½ cup water	1 vanilla bean, split
2½ cups heavy cream	8 egg yolks

1. Combine 1 cup sugar and the water in a small saucepan. Heat to a boil. Using a pastry brush dipped in water, wash down the sides of the pan removing any crystals. Don't stir this mixture with a spoon, simply swirl the pan to blend in any crystals.

2. Cook the syrup to deep golden brown, watching constantly to avoid burning. Remove from the heat and slowly add ⅓ cup cream in a threadlike stream, whisking constantly until the mixture is thoroughly blended. Set aside.

3. In a large saucepan, bring the remaining cream, the milk, and vanilla bean to a boil. In a mixing bowl, whisk the egg yolks and remaining ⅔ cup sugar together.

4. Temper the egg mixture by adding one-third of the hot liquid while whisking constantly, then whisk in the remaining liquid.

5. Return the mixture to the saucepan. Over low heat, stir constantly until the mixture thickens enough to coat the back of a spoon. Stir in the reserved caramel sauce.

4. Strain the custard through a sieve into a bowl placed over ice. Stir as the custard cools. When it is chilled, place in an ice-cream freezer and process according to the manufacturer's instructions. (If you can, chill the custard overnight. The ice cream will be much smoother.)

ADVANCE PREPARATION: Should be made at least 1 day ahead and will keep for 2 weeks in the freezer.

Chocolate-Chestnut Mousse

$\mathcal{W}$e don't ordinarily think that chocolate has a place in the Thanksgiving feast, but the addition of chestnuts makes this rich mousse quite appropriate. We have found that the flavors of this luscious dessert marry more thoroughly if it is refrigerated overnight.

Serves 8

4 tablespoons cocoa	4 tablespoons Amaretto
Two 8¾-ounce cans French chestnut spread	2 cups heavy cream

1. Combine the cocoa and the chestnut spread in a large bowl. Stir in the Amaretto.

2. In another bowl whip the cream until stiff peaks are formed. Fold the cream into the chestnut mixture. Spoon into 8 wineglasses. Refrigerate for at least 3 hours.

NOTE: We use the *crème de marrons* made by Element Faugier, which is widely available, for the canned chestnut spread.

ADVANCE PREPARATION: Should be prepared 1 day ahead. Refrigerate.

Glazed Oranges

$\mathcal{T}$his lively dash of orange brightens up the holiday color scheme.

Serves 12 to 14

12 navel oranges	1 cup sugar
2 cups water	¼ cup crème de cassis

1. Peel the zest of three oranges and chop, making about ¼ cup zest. Cover and reserve in the refrigerator. Peel and cut the pith off all of the oranges with a sharp knife, making sure that none of the white part remains, or the dish will be bitter. The oranges can be left whole or sliced into rounds. If you want to serve this dish immediately, cut into rounds.

2. In a saucepan bring the water and sugar to a boil, then simmer for 5 minutes. Cool for 10 minutes. Add the crème de cassis.

3. Place the oranges in a glass bowl that holds them snugly. Pour the syrup over them and marinate, in the refrigerator, for 4 hours or overnight. (If you have cut the oranges into rounds, the marination can be shortened to 1 hour, but the longer the better.)

4. Before serving sprinkle with the reserved zest.

VARIATIONS: Here are two ways to give the oranges a unique character:

1. Instead of crème de cassis, use 2 tablespoons chopped fresh tarragon and eliminate the 10-minute cooling period in step 2.

2. Add 2 tablespoons grenadine to the crème de cassis syrup to make the fruit look like blood oranges.

ADVANCE PREPARATION: Can be made 1 day ahead. Cover and refrigerate.

Foamy Brandy Sauce

*T*his is a luscious sauce that can add a new dimension to some desserts. We serve it with Persimmon Pudding (see page 178), Jessica's Carmelized Apple Tart (see page 164), Apple Pie (see page 162), or Moosehead Gingerbread (see page 176).

Makes 2½ cups

3 eggs, separated	1 cup heavy cream
¾ cup sugar	1 teaspoon vanilla extract
2 tablespoons unsalted butter, softened	3 tablespoons brandy

1. In a medium bowl, whip the egg yolks and sugar together until thick and light in color. Whisk the butter into the mixture.

2. In another bowl, whip the cream until stiff.

3. In a small bowl, whip the egg whites until stiff but not dry.

4. Fold the egg whites and cream alternately into the egg yolk mixture. Stir in the vanilla and the brandy. Serve chilled.

ADVANCE PREPARATION: Can be kept up to 2 hours in the refrigerator.

Aunt Dink's Penuche Nuts

*A*ndy's Aunt Dinah (her nickname was "Dink") gave us a container of these nuts every year for Thanksgiving. Dink died in 1989 at the age of 95. She was one of the brightest and sweetest people we have ever known. Her wit and intelligence were an important part of many of our Thanksgiving celebrations.

Makes 3 cups

1 cup firmly packed dark brown
   sugar
½ cup granulated sugar
½ cup sour cream

1 teaspoon vanilla extract
2½ cups walnuts

1. Put the sugars and the sour cream into a saucepan, whisking over low heat. Cook until the mixture starts to boil. Cover and boil for 1 minute.

2. Uncover and cook until a few drops of syrup form a firm ball or a candy thermometer reads 245 degrees.

3. Remove from the heat and add the vanilla and the walnuts. Stir to coat evenly.

4. Empty the contents of the saucepan onto wax paper and, with tongs, separate the nuts. Allow them to cool completely. Store in a closed container in a cool place.

ADVANCE PREPARATION: Can be prepared at least 1 week ahead and stored at room temperature.

Leftovers

*F*or many people leftovers are the best part of the holiday experience. This is especially true for those who actually prepare the Thanksgiving feast. There is so much to think about and so much work to do on the day of, that often the host and hostess don't get much of a chance to sit down, relax, and enjoy the moment.

The next day, when everything is cooked, all the guests are gone, and the cleanup has been done, it's much easier to take the time to really appreciate the work of the days before.

Actually, we generally eat our leftovers "as is," warmed to room temperature on Friday. Most of the ingredients of the Thanksgiving feast are hearty and flavorful enough to taste as good if not better the day after. It is one of our best days of the year, the six of us together around the kitchen table, relaxed and happy.

Turkey, if it was not overcooked on Thursday, is excellent on Friday. It is moist and doesn't pick up secondary flavors like some other meats. Stuffing is excellent on the second day and so are most Thanksgiving vegetables. Things that need to be crisp when served—Caitlin's Potatoes and a few other things in the book—lose texture overnight, but desserts are particularly fine the next day.

But this warm aura around the holiday meal is only good up to a point. After eating the Thanksgiving dinner twice, it's time to magically convert it into something else. In our house, anyway, the same food the third time around is a just cause for mutiny. This chapter is here to save you from mass defections from your dinner table.

What follows are some very clever ways to present the same old food in a completely new format.

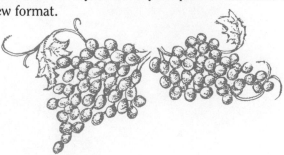

Emmy's Turkey Soup

$\mathcal{E}$mmy Smith was the maid-of-honor at our wedding. She is a talented cook. Emmy, who grew up in Vermont, has enjoyed this delicious post-Thanksgiving soup since she was a little girl. "It's my favorite Thanksgiving dish," she says. This is a "throw together" soup and the ingredients and measurements are only approximate. Let your own leftovers and refrigerator resources dictate the amounts.

Makes enough for 8

1 cut-up turkey carcass
Leftover gravy, stuffing, meat
　　and skin scraps (If the neck
　　and gizzards haven't been
　　used, add them also.)
7 carrots
3 leeks, sliced
2 cups coarsely chopped celery,
　　including leaves
4 boiling potatoes
A small handful of fresh parsley

6 crushed peppercorns
Cold water or stock
2 parsnips, peeled and sliced
　　into rounds
18 white pearl onions, peeled
　　(see step 1, page 90)
12 mushrooms, quartered and
　　previously sautéed
3 cups cut-up leftover turkey
1 package frozen peas
Salt and freshly ground pepper

1. Put the carcass, leftovers, 4 coarsely chopped carrots, leeks, celery, 2 peeled and halved potatoes, parsley, and peppercorns in a large soup pot. Cover with cold water (or stock, if you want a richer soup) and bring to a boil. Lower heat and simmer, uncovered, for 3 to 4 hours, skimming frequently.

2. Pour through a strainer into a large bowl. Press down on the solids to extract all liquid. Refrigerate until the fat has risen to the top and solidified enough to remove easily with a spoon.

3. Slice the remaining 3 carrots into rounds, and peel and quarter the remaining 2 potatoes. Return the broth to the soup pot, bring to a simmer, and add the carrots, potatoes, and all remaining ingredients, except the peas.

4. Simmer, uncovered, for 1 hour. Just before serving, add the peas. Adjust seasoning and serve piping hot, accompanied by crusty bread.

Toby's Instant Replay Sandwich

*O*ur son, Toby, loves Thanksgiving dinner so much that he has invented a way to reprise the pleasures of the meal in one quick, no fuss package. This overstuffed (no pun intended) sandwich is one of the greatest pleasures of the holiday weekend.

Makes 1 sandwich

2 ¾-inch slices of brioche, challah, or other egg bread
2 tablespoons leftover gravy
½ cup leftover stuffing

2 or 3 slices cooked turkey breast
¼ cup cranberry condiment

1. Spread both slices of bread with 1 tablespoon of gravy.
2. Evenly distribute the stuffing over one slice of bread. Lay the turkey meat on top and then spread the cranberries evenly on top of the turkey. Top with the other bread slice. Cut in half. Serve.

Open-Face Turkey Sandwich

*H*ere's a quick way to make a dramatic dish out of leftover turkey. We like this for Saturday lunch, when the bird is starting to get a little tired. This saucy preparation will revitalize a sagging turkey.

Makes 1 sandwich

One ¾-inch-thick slice bread from a crusty, round country loaf (We prefer sourdough, if available.)
1 clove garlic
1 tablespoon olive oil
1 shallot, minced
¼ cup white wine

¼ cup leftover gravy
1 small celery stalk, minced
Salt and freshly ground black pepper
3 or 4 slices cooked white turkey meat
Chopped fresh parsley

1. Toast the bread in an oven until hard. Cut the garlic clove in half lengthwise and rub the bread with the cut side.

2. In a skillet, heat the olive oil and sauté the shallot until it is soft, not brown. Add the wine and reduce to 1 tablespoon. Add the gravy and celery. Season to taste, but remember that the gravy is already pretty highly seasoned.

3. When the sauce is heated through, add the turkey slices to warm through, about 1 minute.

4. Place the toast on a plate, top with the turkey slices, and spoon the remaining sauce over the sandwich. Finish with chopped parsley and serve immediately.

Turkey and Rice Casserole

$\mathcal{A}$ nother kid pleaser, this adaptation of *arroz con pollo* is easy and a real winner.

Serves 6 to 8

5 tablespoons butter	3 tablespoons minced fresh
3 cloves garlic, minced	parsley
2 medium onions, peeled and	½ teaspoon fresh thyme
diced	Salt and freshly ground pepper
3 cups diced cooked turkey	1 cup long-grain rice
1 cup stuffing	2 cups Chicken (see page 77)
	or Turkey Stock (see page 78)

1. Preheat the oven to 375 degrees. In the bottom of a 4-quart oven-proof casserole, melt 4 tablespoons butter over medium heat and sauté the garlic and onions until transparent, about 5 minutes. Add the turkey, stuffing, and herbs, and season to taste with salt and pepper. Stir.

2. In a saucepan, melt the remaining tablespoon of butter. Add the rice and sauté over medium heat until it is transparent.

3. Add the rice to the casserole. Stir to mix. Bring the broth to a boil in a saucepan and pour it over the casserole. Cover and bake for 25 minutes, until the rice is tender. Uncover and bake 15 more minutes. Serve.

Turkey Mornay

*H*ere's an excellent way to convert leftover turkey into a rich and elegant dish.

Serves 4

1½ cups heavy cream
3 cups ½-inch-dice cooked
  turkey meat

½ teaspoon freshly ground white
  pepper

MORNAY SAUCE

2 tablespoons unsalted butter
2 tablespoons all-purpose flour
1 cup hot milk
1 teaspoon salt

1 small onion, thinly sliced
2 egg yolks
5 tablespoons grated Parmesan
  cheese

1. In a medium skillet bring the cream to a boil over medium heat. Reduce heat and simmer, stirring frequently, for 20 minutes, or until the cream is reduced to about 1 cup. Stir in the turkey and the pepper. Continue to simmer for 5 minutes. Set aside.

2. To make the sauce: Melt the butter in a 2-quart saucepan over medium heat and stir in the flour. Continue stirring until the mixture is golden, about 3 minutes.

3. Add the milk, salt, and onion. Stirring constantly, simmer about 5 minutes, or until the sauce begins to bubble. Pour through a fine sieve into a bowl and discard the onion.

4. Return the sauce to the saucepan. Whisk in the egg yolks and 3 tablespoons of Parmesan.

5. Transfer the turkey mixture to an 8½ by 5½ by 1½-inch au gratin dish or an 8-inch glass pie plate. Pour the mornay sauce over the turkey, and sprinkle the top with the remaining Parmesan.

6. Place under the broiler about 5 inches from the heat. Cook until lightly browned, about 45 seconds. Serve immediately.

Killer Turkey Hash

So it's the day after and there you are with a lot of dirty dishes, a cranberry stain on the new rug, and about 10 pounds of leftover turkey. What to do with it? Yes, you can make sandwiches, but then it might take until Christmas to polish off the bird. No, you have to come up with a main course dish that will consume a big chunk of turkey all at once. One excellent suggestion is turkey hash—a delicious dish that everyone loves and a recipe in which you can vary the ingredients at will and still create a culinary triumph.

Serves 6 to 8

2 tablespoons unsalted butter
1 onion, chopped
2 garlic cloves, minced
3 cups ¼-inch-dice cooked
   turkey
3 cups crumbled stuffing or
   ¼-inch-dice boiled potatoes
1 cup leftover gravy

¾ cup cooked corn
2 tablespoons minced fresh
   parsley
1 teaspoon salt
Freshly ground pepper
3 eggs, well beaten
¾ cup grated Parmesan cheese
4 tablespoons bread crumbs

1. Melt the butter in a skillet and sauté the onion and garlic until transparent, stirring frequently with a wooden spoon. Add the turkey and stuffing, stirring to blend. Add the gravy, corn, parsley, salt, and pepper to taste.

2. In a small bowl combine the eggs and cheese. Preheat the broiler.

3. Transfer the turkey mixture to a 2-quart soufflé dish, casserole, or au gratin dish. Add the egg and cheese mixture. Stir to combine all ingredients. Sprinkle the top of the hash with bread crumbs.

4. Place the hash under the broiler until the bread crumbs begin to brown, about 7 minutes. Serve immediately.

VARIATIONS: Substitute or add any combination of the following: walnuts, water chestnuts, pecans, black olives, cooked broccoli or other vegetables, bacon, ham, or pork sausage.

Turkey Tortilla Casserole

*A*mong a stellar group of leftover creations, this dish is the champion. At least it is a sensation with our kids. The first time we tested this recipe we left it in the kitchen for about 10 minutes and returned to find Jessica, our very fussy 15-year-old, camped over the casserole. Half of it had been eaten.

The recipe came to us by way of Barbara Goldie, one of San Francisco's most charming hostesses.

Serves 12

3 cups ½-inch-dice cooked white turkey meat
1 quart Tamale Sauce
½ cup sliced pitted black olives
¾ cup chunky-style tomato sauce (Use a 15-ounce can and reserve the remainder for Tamale Sauce opposite.)
¼ teaspoon freshly ground pepper
⅛ teaspoon cayenne
1 teaspoon chili powder
1½ cups fresh corn, blanched for 3 minutes, or frozen corn, defrosted

1 red bell pepper, diced and sautéed for 3 minutes in 1 tablespoon olive oil
1 teaspoon sugar
2 teaspoons Worcestershire sauce
1 pound tortilla chips (Use thick and crisp triangular corn chips that are actually made from cut tortillas, not the orange extruded ones made by the big commercial companies.)
½ cup grated Jalisco or Monterey Jack cheese

1. Preheat the oven to 350 degrees. Mix all the ingredients except the chips and cheese in a bowl. Pour into a 15 by 10-inch Pyrex baking dish. Stud the casserole with the chips. Bake in the preheated oven for 30 minutes.

2. Sprinkle the top of the casserole with the cheese. Return to the oven until the cheese is melted. Serve immediately.

Tamale Sauce

Makes 1 quart

1½ cups Mexican-style red chili sauce
⅔ cup chunky-style tomato sauce
3 cups Chicken Stock (see page 77)

1 teaspoon chili powder
6 tablespoons unsalted butter
¼ cup masa harina or white cornmeal

1. Mix the sauces, chicken stock, and chili powder in a bowl. Reserve.

2. Melt the butter in a large skillet over medium heat and add the cornmeal. Cook for 3 minutes. Mix in the sauce mixture. Stir until thick, about 5 minutes.

NOTE: This sauce can be made a few days in advance of Thanksgiving and refrigerated. The day after, when you are tired, this dish should take only a few minutes to assemble.

Curried Turkey Salad

*T*his is so good that it would be worth cooking an extra turkey just to have it. (In fact, we have been known to cook a whole turkey breast, chill it, and cut it up for the sole purpose of making this salad. It is a perfect warm weather lunch dish.)

Makes 5 cups

2 cups 2-inch-strips cooked white turkey meat
½ cup blanched, slivered almonds
½ cup halved lengthwise white seedless grapes
2 scallions sliced in ⅛-inch rounds

2 stalks of celery, cut into small dice
¼ cup chopped Major Grey chutney
1 tablespoon curry powder
1 cup mayonnaise
Salt and freshly ground pepper

1. In a bowl, combine the turkey, almonds, grapes, scallions, and celery.

2. In another bowl, combine the chutney, curry powder, and mayonnaise. Stir well. Add this mixture to the turkey mixture and toss with two forks to blend. Season. Serve on a bed of lettuce. This is also attractive as a sandwich filling.

Goose Ragout

*Y*ou couldn't ask for a simpler recipe than this, and the result is nothing short of sensational. This ragout is particularly delicious made with goose and Savory Wild Rice Stuffing (page 71), but it would work almost as well with turkey or other poultry. The proportions can be varied.

Makes 6 cups

3 cups goose meat, from the legs, wings, and the carcass, cut into ¾-inch chunks, turkey (preferably dark meat), or chicken

3 cups rice-based stuffing
2 cups Goose Pan Gravy (see page 80)
Salt and freshly ground pepper

Wine and
Other Beverages

*T*he leaves have turned a lovely spectrum of earth colors; there's a crisp, cool stillness to the night air; and in the afternoon you can hear the snap of footballs and the crunch of shoulder pads. The time has come to plan the holiday feast and, once again, to consider that most difficult of gustatory enigmas: What wine should be served with the Thanksgiving turkey?

There are many unanswered questions that puzzle mankind. What is the meaning of life? Who was better, Mays or Mantle? Is there anyone who really likes poi? Among the most troublesome of these questions is the age-old which-wine-with-turkey quandary.

At the first Thanksgiving there was no wine at all. The Pilgrim fathers followed an exigent credo that equated almost everything pleasurable with sin. Thus there was no wine. There also had been no attempt to plant vineyards during the colonists' first months in America. Contemporary Americans have adopted a moderate but far more positive attitude toward pleasure than the Puritans, and wine is near the top of the list of pleasures.

The turkey dinner cries out for wine. Its assertive and complicated flavors need a unifying background, a carefully orchestrated theme that ties all of its diverse elements together. So, the choice of wine moves front and center, and a difficult, complicated choice it is.

"Wait a minute," says the wine maven. "I have the answer. Ever since I was old enough to sit on my father's knee he told me that everything I needed to know in life was summed up in these simple words: 'White with fish and white meat; red with red meat and game.' "

Well, turkey is white meat. So, therefore, if we are being dogmatic, a white wine should be served. Right? Not necessarily. If the Thanksgiving dinner were nothing more than a few slices of breast meat and a nondescript vegetable, then a simple white wine definitely would be the answer.

But Thanksgiving is much more than that. In fact, the turkey may be the blandest and most neutral part of the feast. (Unless, of course, we are talking about dark meat, which changes everything again.) Think about it.

At most Thanksgiving celebrations the turkey is only one element in a parade of aggressively flavored foods.

It is important to think beyond the bird and try to pick the right wine to go with chestnut stuffing, creamed onions, root vegetable purée, sweet potatoes, and three different kinds of cranberry sauce.

This cacophony of intense flavors requires a wine of more than subtle charms. Whatever is chosen to accompany a dinner of such complexity will certainly have to have a balancing, assertive flavor. But it should definitely not be a venerable, aged wine. The nuances of maturity would be obliterated by the pugnacious and uncomplicated flavors of the Thanksgiving feast.

So where does this leave us? If the wine is to be white, it must have intensity, structure, and richness. It has to hold its own against flavors that are alternately salty, fruity, spicy, and rich. If the wine is to be white it should be a husky, barrel-fermented Sauvignon Blanc, a vigorous Gewurztraminer, or America's favorite white—Chardonnay. But it shouldn't be just any Chardonnay. To stand up to the meal it must be a powerful wine with ripe fruit, firm acidity, and rich, toasty oak.

But what about red? Red wines have been gaining in popularity lately as more and more Americans discover their considerable charms. A red might be just the ticket for the holiday repast, but which ones would work? Quite a few. Pinot Noir is ideal, we have found, because it has plenty of fruit and rich flavor, yet it is still a noble wine that is appropriate for an important occasion.

We are such Pinot Noir and Burgundy lovers that we usually look for any small excuse to parade out favorites from Beaune or the Carneros. Actually, we have discovered that these wines are excellent and almost ideal with the harvest feast. Their flavors are forward enough without being coarse and their cherry and plum fruitiness nicely complements all of the predominant Thanksgiving flavors. We have been serving Pinot Noir wines at our Thanksgiving dinners over the past six years and they have been enormously popular with our guests.

Beaujolais wines are another very good solution. The fresh new "Primeur" wines from France are released around November 20, just in time for Thanksgiving. These wines are bright and fruity with lots of charm and plenty of lively acidity. For people who are expecting to drink white wines, these engaging reds are an ideal compromise since they are delicious when served slightly chilled. Frankly, regular Beaujolais wines of recent vintages —those from Fleurie, Julienas, Chiroubles, and Morgon in particular—are even better because they are generally more substantial than the typical "Nouveau" wine.

Another ideal wine for Thanksgiving is Zinfandel. This lush and lively red is a perfect match for cranberry sauce and giblet gravy. A good Zin has smooth, velvety texture and ripe raspberry fruit that complements the big flavors of the holiday feast.

Also appropriate would be Syrah and other Rhone-type wines. These big reds have luscious, broad flavors that wrap themselves around the earthy, rich textures and tastes of Thanksgiving. If you feel strongly that the wines for the most American of holidays should be American, there is a whole new crop of California wines made by some very talented young vintners who call themselves "The Rhone Rangers." These wineries produce fruity red wines from Grenache, Syrah, and Mourvedre, some of the best varieties grown in the Rhone Valley of southeastern France.

If you don't mind being just a little un-American, some crisp Italian reds such as Chianti, Valpolicella, Dolcetto, and certain younger Barbarescos do very well on the Thanksgiving table. These wines have the richness, fruit, and complexity that you would expect from a red wine, but they also have bright, tangy acid that makes them similar to white wines.

You may have noticed that we have not mentioned Cabernet Sauvignon or Merlot. We have found that these wines, with their herbal character, often conflict with the flavors of Thanksgiving. Their subtleties and complexities also tend to get lost in the variety of tones and textures that the holiday feast provides.

Another type of wine that can be appropriate for the holiday fete is "blush" or blanc de noir. These often have a touch more intensity and depth than many white wines, but they still have the fruitiness of whites and can be served chilled. We would caution you to look for blush wines that are crisp and close to dry. Wines that are too sweet will conflict with many of the traditional Thanksgiving flavors.

As you can probably tell, our first choice for a holiday wine would be a red, most likely a Pinot Noir. But there are many other possibilities and some of them are white and some of them are pink.

Actually, we usually start with cold champagne or California sparkling wine with appetizers in the living room. We generally choose a crisp, light blanc de blanc, a wine made entirely from white grapes, in most cases all Chardonnay. Although we think it is important to have American wines at Thanksgiving, we sometimes sneak in a bottle or two of our favorite French champagnes.

One year we poured Chardonnay for the preprandial festivities, and we chose a crisp, lively wine—not a big oaky monster.

At table, guests find a few bottles of red already opened. We like to present wines from various wineries, but we always make the choices

within the type we have selected. For instance, we like Pinot Noir, so we will pick four Pinots, all from the same year but from wineries in four different counties.

With dessert we like to return to sparkling wine, this time choosing a softer wine with a higher *dosage* (sugar content) such as a *cremant* or a luscious rosé.

Most Americans drink white wines too cold and red wines too warm. In warmer weather it is quite acceptable to chill Chardonnays and other whites, but too much cold will shut down their flavor. Keep them at around 55 degrees, no less. A half hour in the refrigerator is time enough to cool your wine; more than that will take the edge off the flavor.

As for reds, it is perfectly okay to pop them into the refrigerator for ten minutes or so. Beaujolais and Zinfandel are particularly good when cooled down to 60 or 65 degrees. A slight chill can add a refreshing dimension to other reds too, but don't get carried away.

But there are other drinks besides wine. For teetotalers at our Thanksgiving table we like to offer sparkling apple cider and sparkling mineral water. Both of these are refreshing and help with the digestion of this rich meal.

Finally there is beer. Actually, beer is quite good with Thanksgiving dinner, but we would suggest a fairly full-flavored beer, perhaps even an ale. Some of the darker, sweeter imports are very compatible with the holiday trimmings.

In any case, the choice of beverages is an important one. Wines and other drinks require some thought and should be an early part of your planning procedure. A good glass of wine can be the thing that turns a good dinner into a great one.

Index